HISTORIC C
OF ENGLAND

CW01604803

HISTORIC CITIES OF ENGLAND

Photographed by
ERNEST FRANKL

THE PEVENSEY PRESS
Cambridge England

Published by The Pevensey Press
6 De Freville Avenue, Cambridge CB4 1HR, UK

© Ernest Frankl and the Pevensey Press, 1988

ISBN 0 907115 37 3 hard covers
0 907115 paperback

Acknowledgements
Photographs by Ernest Frankl except **5**, Cambridge University Collection of Aerial Photographs; **12**, The Royal Pavilion, Art Gallery and Museums, Brighton; **37**, Edward Leigh, courtesy of the Provost and Fellows of King's College; **42**, Edward Leigh, courtesy of the Master and Fellows of Trinity College; **61**, Howard Moore, Woodmansterne Ltd; **62**, Nicholas Servian, Woodmansterne Ltd; **95**, Holte Photographics Ltd, courtesy of the Royal Shakespeare Company; **103**, Woodmansterne Ltd.

Permission to reproduce the following photographs is gratefully acknowledged; **23**, The Revd Edwin A. Morris, Rector of the City of Bristol; **27**, The Vicar and Churchwarden of St Mary Redcliffe, Bristol; **28**, The Very Revd A. H. Dammers, Dean of Bristol; **49, 50, 51**, the Dean and Chapter of Canterbury; **104, 105**, the Dean and Chapter of Winchester.

Designed by Jim Reader

Jacket design by Kate Hughes-Stanton

Design and production in association with
Book Production Consultants, Cambridge

Typesetting in Baskerville by Cambridge Photosetting Services
Printed in Hong Kong

Front cover Bath from Widcombe Hill.

Half title Bootham Bar, the well-fortified entrance to York from the north of England, dating from the 11th century, contains some of the oldest masonry in the fortifications which still encircle the city.

Frontispiece The east front of Hampton Court Palace, seen from Broad Walk. This extension to the original Tudor palace was designed by Christopher Wren and built 1689–94. The range shown here is occupied by the Queen's apartments.

Back cover Buckingham Palace from St James's Park.

Contents

Bath 6
by Paul Newman & Marianne Brace

Brighton 21
by Angela Fiddes & Marianne Brace

Bristol 31
by Paul Newman & T. V. Buttrey

Cambridge 43
by Michael Hall & Marianne Brace

Canterbury 59
by T. V. Buttrey

London 69
by Michael Hall

Oxford 91
by Michael Hall & Marianne Brace

Stratford-upon-Avon 107
by Michael Hall & Marianne Brace

Winchester 116
by Colin Badcock & T. V. Buttrey

York 129
by Angela Fiddes & Marianne Brace

Bath

For centuries people have sought refreshment in Bath: a cure for physical ills, a tonic for flagging spirits. Today the town still has the power to revivify with its honey-coloured buildings, mineral waters and tea-rooms.

Bath's architectural style dates from the 18th century, when it became a fashionable spa. But the benefits of its natural springs had been enjoyed long before, by the Romans, who colonised Britain in AD43.

The principal spring was already devoted to a Celtic deity, Sulis, and the Romans dedicated its soothing waters to Minerva, their goddess of healing and wisdom. Carvings of both deities are displayed in the **Roman Baths Museum**. Sulis, wild-eyed and tangle-haired, formed the centrepiece of a pediment crowning the temple built above the spring in the gods' joint honour. Other vestiges of the Roman occupation of Aquae Sulis – as Bath was known – include mosaics, coins and pewterware.

The water is full of iron and stains the ground red, as you see at the sacred spring overflow (**1**), where it rushes from a rock-opening belching steam and stinking of sulphur. The museum feels a bit like a sauna at this point, as 250,000 gallons of water surge up daily at a temperature of 46.5°C.

The Romans piped this warm water into several baths lined with lead, and heated the complex with underfloor hot-air channels. Parts of this hypocaust are still visible. From the museum you emerge into the daylight alongside the **Great Bath**, which was once covered by a timber roof. It was the Victorians who erected the Roman-style colonnades and statues that now surround the bath. The original patrons lounged by the gently steaming water, being massaged or plunging into the nearby circular **Cold Bath**.

Through an arch you glimpse the bubbling green water of the enclosed **King's Bath**, situated over the great reservoir fed by the springs. Above it, in a niche, sits Bladud, legendary son of a Celtic king of the 8th century BC. Afflicted with leprosy, Bladud spent his exile as a swineherd and discovered the medicinal nature of the springs when a swim healed his sores.

The water later gained a reputation for fertility. Queen Anne, wife of James I, witnessed its powers of generation – not, unfortunately, the ones she expected – when the King's Bath spontaneously combusted and a flame shot across the water's surface. However, Mary, wife of James II, *did* conceive after immersing herself at Hot Bath Street in **Cross Bath** – so called, some say, because a cross was erected in 1688 to commemorate the occasion. Others believe the bath dates back at least to 1302. A dip here looks extremely uninviting and was probably no less so in the 17th century. One visitor criticised the town's filthy streets, its slimy walls and the refuse in the water. Pepys braved the King's Bath despite the scum which was raked off daily because it caused pimples and rashes.

It was Queen Anne's patronage, in the 18th century, which cleaned up

1 *Each day in Bath 250,000 gallons of water rush from underground at a temperature of 46.5°C. This is the overflow from the Romans' sacred spring and reservoir into the outfall drain, which led to the river.*

OVERLEAF
2 *Bath from Widcombe Hill.*

Bath's image. Visitors flooded in and, according to the writer Daniel Defoe, with the sick came the healthy in order to commit the worst of all murders: 'to kill time'.

The meeting place was the **Grand Pump Room**. Designed in 1706 and added to in 1784, it overlooks the King's Bath on one side and Abbey Church Yard on the other. Its motto, 'Water is Best', is shown in Greek on the exterior entablature.

Notable residents who probably consumed the pump water included the novelists Fanny Burney, who lived at 14 South Parade, and Jane Austen, who stayed at 4 Sydney Place; General Wolfe, who had an especially charming

house at 5 Trim Street; and 'Beau' Nash, the famous Master of Ceremonies and self-styled king of the spa. His house, next to the Theatre Royal, is now Popjoys Restaurant, named after Nash's mistress, Juliana Papjoy.

For a small sum today's visitors can sample the water. The recommended dose was three glasses, but finishing one is hard enough. Slightly radioactive and unpleasantly tepid, it tastes as if eggs have been boiling in it. Much more delicious is tea sipped to the strains of the Pump Room Trio or a meal savoured in the adjoining Concert Room or on the terrace overlooking the Great Bath and **Abbey** (**3**).

The full authority of this magnificent building is best appreciated from the **Abbey Church Yard**, which links the Roman city (baths, springs and museum) with the medieval one (the church). Here, in summer, shops and colonnades are adorned with bright hanging baskets, and buskers perform to passers-by and pigeons.

Fire destroyed the original church on this site in 1137. Later in the 12th century the Bishop of Bath gave the impoverished townspeople access to the waters by founding **St John's Hospital**, hidden away in Chapel Courtyard. It remains the town's oldest charity. Around the corner in St James's Parade looms the sole notable remnant of Elizabethan Bath: **Abbey Church House** (visits by appointment only).

In 1499 the Abbey Church was redesigned in a Perpendicular Gothic style. The west front's carved turrets depict the vision which inspired Bishop Oliver King to undertake the renovation. Dreaming that he wandered in the old church ruins, the Bishop saw the Holy Trinity and a ladder with angels. Crowned at the base was an olive tree. A voice, punning on his name, commanded 'Let an olive establish the crown and a king restore the church.'

With the dissolution of the monasteries in 1539 the Abbey Church again

3 Above: *Bath Abbey from the south-west.*

4 Right: *Sally Lunn's House.*

OVERLEAF
5 *The Circus and Crescents from the air.*

The oldest house in Bath 1482
SALLY LUNN
lived here
1680

6 Left: *A detail of the Circus.*

7 Above: *The splendid Banqueting Room of Bath's Guildhall (1766–78).*

needed repair. Bishop Montague (whose tomb lies in the north aisle) decided to take the initiative when sheltering from the rain beneath its leaky roof with a companion who remarked 'How, if the church does not save us from the water above, can it save us from the fire below?' The Bishop's brother, Sir Henry Montague, donated the carved west doors in 1617.

Thanks to 52 windows and an unbroken view from west to east, the interior is blissfully light, deserving its description as 'the lantern of England'. The roof is fan-vaulted and the walls clad in the 18th-century memorial tablets of those who travelled from as far as Jersey, Scotland and Tipperary seeking a cure.

Behind the Abbey in **Orange Grove** an obelisk commemorates a visit by William of Orange in 1734. A second in Queen Square honours Prince Frederick, and a third, situated in the lower western part of **Victoria Park**, records the highlights of Queen Victoria's career.

Thomas Baldwin, who was responsible for the colonnaded walkway between Stall and Bath Streets, also designed the **Guildhall**, north of the Abbey. Its fine banqueting room (**7**) can be viewed on weekdays. Alongside is the covered **Market**, where vendors have gathered since medieval times. A hundred years ago it was frequented by such characters as Guinea Pig Jack and his performing rodents, Farmer One-Cow, who grazed a solitary beast, and Punch Newton, a police sergeant who refused to make arrests.

A sycamore dominates **Abbey Green**. Of the monastery once standing here all that remains is a single hinge set into the wall of St Michael's Arch. Picturesque streets beckon. In North Parade Passage, originally Lilliput Alley, stands **Sally Lunn's House** (**4**). Built in the 15th century and refashioned in the 17th, its name comes from a cake-seller and it is now,

OVERLEAF
8 *The Royal Crescent.*

appropriately, a tea-shop. The special flat 'Sally Lunn' buns are served here, and the original ovens can be seen in the basement.

Bath's streets are walled rather than paved with gold – the local stone which ensures that all the buildings harmonise, whatever their period. It was the 18th-century architect John Wood who put it to such excellent use when he envisaged a new Roman city of noble buildings joined in graceful terraces, crescents and squares. The best examples of his work are **Queen Square** (**10**) and, in the upper town, the **Circus** (**6**), completed by his son. Steep **Gay Street** connects the two. From the top you have a splendid view of the encroaching wooded hills.

The honey-coloured buildings of the Circus are characterised by Greek columns on each floor: Doric on the ground, Ionic above and Corinthian on top. The painter Gainsborough lived at No. 17, and would have looked on to a cobbled central area rather than the plane trees and grass seen today.

Bennett Street leads away in one direction to the **Upper Assembly Rooms and Costume Museum**, where tea dances have replaced the concerts and card games offered to the 18th-century *beau monde*. In the other direction, past **Margaret's Buildings**, a pedestrian precinct of antiques shops and cafés, spreads the **Royal Crescent** (**8**), conceived by John Wood the Younger. Despite the softening effect of the park rolling away below it, this formal curve of buildings is breathtakingly grand. In 1772 Elizabeth Linley eloped from No. 11 with the playwright Sheridan. Now most of the houses contain flats, except No. 1, which is authentically furnished and open to the public.

The crescent was supposedly inspired by Bernini's colonnade surrounding

9 Below: *Pulteney Bridge from the river.*

10 Above: *Queen Square (1726–36), John Wood the Elder's first major development in Bath. Wood himself lived on the north side, shown here.*

the Piazza S. Pietro in Rome. In the lower town, spanning the River Avon, **Pulteney Bridge** (**9**) also suggests an Italian influence. Completed in 1774 by Robert Adam, shops line its elegant walkways and overlook the weir below. North-east of the bridge the road becomes **Great Pulteney Street**, an imposing thoroughfare where many famous people lodged – such as the statesman Lord Macaulay and the great reformer William Wilberforce.

Descend to the river here and you can admire the Empire Hotel and floral **Parade Gardens** on the opposite bank; or follow the river down towards Bath Spa Station and amble back along the rural towpath of the Kennet and Avon Canal, past the sloping allotments, locks and long-boats of people whose home is the water itself.

Brighton

11 *Brighton Pavilion, remodelled by John Nash for the Prince Regent (later George IV) in 1815. The oriental colonnade, the 'jalis' of pierced stone latticework, the cornice of Indian battlements, the domes and the minarets encase what was originally a Palladian building.*

OVERLEAF

12 Left: *The climax of the Pavilion's interior transformation: the opulent chinoiserie of the Banqueting Room, chiefly designed by Robert Jones.*

13 Right: *Brunswick Square, begun in 1824 in what was then the tiny village of Hove. Amon Wilds and C. A. Busby were responsible for the designs and for much of the new building which took place in the 1820s, when Brighton spread as the number of visitors increased.*

The first stop for visitors to Brighton should be the sea. Stretching out turquoise-blue (if you are lucky), it has a bearing on everything worth seeing in the town.

Recorded in the Domesday Book (1086), Brighton began as a fishing settlement called Bristelmestune; St Nicholas of Myra was its patron saint, as he is of all fishermen. In the 14th century a church was dedicated to him and set on an isolated hill as a landmark for sailors. Today the **Church of St Nicholas** is landlocked by other buildings but its flinty grey exterior still suggests a hardiness able to withstand the onslaught of salty sea winds. Even the wooden ceiling is like the upturned hull of a ship. The 12th-century font of Caen stone depicts scenes from the New Testament and the life of the saint: in one, a seaborne Nicholas saves pilgrims from the devil.

Buried outside is Phoebe Hassell, who disguised herself as a soldier and followed her lover to the West Indies, keeping her male persona for 17 years. Later the Prince Regent granted her a weekly half-guinea pension. She died aged 108. Here too is the tomb of the architect responsible for many of Brighton's terraces, Amon Wilds. Opposite the porch a modest memorial recalls the actress Dame Flora Robson, who lived in Brighton.

No other medieval buildings survive. But you get an inkling of what Brighton was like by wandering in **The Lanes** (**17**). Demarcated by East, West and North Streets, the centre of the old town is a mesh of dark alleys. The area known as the 'Hempshares' lay between Middle and East Streets; here hemp was grown for fishermen's nets. Today those fishermen would be amazed by the bustling antiques and clothes shops but might approve of the restaurants offering fish specialities or oyster bars like English's in Market Street (**14**). The buildings, mostly 19th century, have over-hanging top storeys, making the narrow streets seem narrower still. According to local legend a fat man once challenged an athlete to a race here and his 10-yard start and alley-route helped him win because his opponent could not overtake. This narrowness, however, nearly tumbled a king.

In 1637 the future Charles II, defeated by Parliamentary forces at the Battle of Worcester, fled to Brighton where a friend, Captain Tettersal (buried in St Nicholas' churchyard), was to ferry him to France. According to local legend, Charles was carried piggy-back by a fisherman down Black Lion Lane, which is only about a yard wide in places. *En route* they met a stout woman. Unable to pass her, and not daring to turn back, the fisherman knocked her down and climbed over, bearing his royal burden to safety.

Ship Street (built on the Hempshares) takes its name from Brighton's oldest inn, the Old Ship Hotel, first recorded in 1559. Across it runs Duke Street. No. 37a dates from 1780 and has a boarded front, unusual in Brighton. A fishing family lived here and their curing house stood in the same

courtyard. The cellar still retains the slate floor where fish were gutted.

Nets were dried and boats beached in The Steine area, but in the 18th century fish gave way to fashion as houses sprang up in **Old Steine** to accommodate sea-bathing visitors. This craze began when Dr Richard Russell from nearby Lewes published a book recommending sea water (for both swimming in and drinking) as a cure for glandular complaints. Few knew how to swim and so employed 'bathers' or 'dippers', like Smoaker Miles (the Prince Regent's dipper) and the celebrated Martha Gunn, to plunge them into the water from the steps of a bathing machine, often early in the day, even in winter. (Martha Gunn's grave is also in St Nicholas' churchyard.)

Some of these elegant houses still exist, such as Marlborough House (now the British Tourist Board office), built in 1769 and possessing a Robert Adam interior, and Steine House (now the YMCA) designed in 1804 for Mrs Fitzherbert, a twice-widowed Roman Catholic who became the Prince Regent's illicit wife. But the most celebrated of all is the whimsical **Royal Pavilion** (**11**), which rises above its neighbours in a cluster of mosque-like domes, minarets and lacy stonework.

The Pavilion's first owner, the Prince Regent (later George IV), is associated with the town's heyday and his bronze statue by Sir Francis Chantrey (1828) poses by the Pavilion's North Gate. Sea-bathing and a visit to his uncle, the Duke of Cumberland, brought George to Brighton; enamoured, he returned yearly. Brighton found him a generous patron and his birthday was celebrated with bell-ringing, a roast ox, races and a ball. It was

14 Above left: *English's Oyster Bar, the celebrated fish restaurant at the entrance to the narrow alleyway of Market Street.*

15 Above right: *The West Pier, designed by Eusebius Birch and opened in 1868, was one of the first piers in Britain. It was a great success, attracting large numbers of visitors, besides providing a landing place for steamers. In the early 1890s the addition of new landing stages and a concert hall nearly doubled its size.*

16 Right: *The West Pier from the Palace Pier.*

DANGER

The Buttercup Boutique
THE PRINT SHOP
STONESHO
47
Drakes of Brighton
JEWELLERS
BRIGHTON SQUARE

17 Left: *Meeting House Lane, in the centre of old Brighton, takes its name from the Friends' Meeting House, which was built here in 1800.*

18 Above: *Brighton beach first thing in the morning, with only a few hardy swimmers taking an early dip. Although it is mainly shingle, this 7-mile beach has always been one of the main attractions of Brighton and Hove, and on sunny days it quickly fills up with people of all ages, building sand castles, paddling, taking boats out, swimming, water-skiing, windsurfing, or just sitting in deck chairs sunbathing.*

here too that the Prince enjoyed time with Maria Fitzherbert. But it was not only Mrs Fitzherbert's company which made Brighton so entertaining. In his room in the Marine Pavilion (the nucleus of the present building) the Prince installed a reflecting glass allowing him to watch the passers-by on the Steine without shifting from his bed.

From the Pavilion Gardens you see William Porden's domed stables (1805), topped by a cupola – a building inspired by the Cornmarket in Paris and Delhi's Great Mosque. Alongside is the Riding House for exercising horses, now an exhibition hall. Once his animals were so grandly housed (better than himself, some whispered), the Prince decided to improve his home with the aid of the architect John Nash. He gave the Pavilion its Indian flavour, adding domes, minarets and colonnades of columns linked by pierced stone latticework.

The interior is quite as extraordinary as the exterior. Chinoiserie dominates rooms of aquamarine, pink, crimson and gold. Here columns are crowned with fake palm leaves; there gilt serpents writhe above stained-glass windows. This opulence comes to a climax in the domed Banqueting Room (**12**), designed by Robert Jones. When William IV succeeded George he added the South and North Lodges, North Gate and Queen Adelaide's Stables in Church Street. The last, now a gallery and museum, has a splendid oriental foyer.

The town is commonly described as Regency though most houses went up later, between 1820 and 1830. Several of Brighton's squares are the combined work of Amon Wilds and C.A. Busby, who created **Marine Parade**. Creamy white houses like those in **Regency Square** and **Brunswick Square** (**13**) (west along Marine Parade) are characteristic, and the squares face out to sea. The architecture may be grand but the slightly weathered quality of the buildings makes even the sweepingly smart **Lewes Crescent** (part of the Kemp Town development, east along Marine Parade) seem friendly rather than forbidding. And not all Brighton's houses are white. **Royal Crescent** (**19**), for example, is distinguished by black 'mathematical' tiles (the origin of the tiles' name is uncertain).

Queen Victoria visited the town too but found it 'a prison'. She left for the last time in 1845, and removed furniture from the Pavilion. The Palace's future looked bleak. Fortunately the Town Commissioners saved it from demolition by buying it for £50,000, a fraction of what the Prince had spent. The royal family has loaned back the fixtures and fittings.

With the Chain Pier (1823), the first pier in Britain, came pleasures of a new kind. Intended as a landing stage for packet boats, it proved a popular venue, especially with William IV, who strolled here and bought sweets for the children who followed him. In 1896 it was closed; two months later it collapsed in a storm. The **Palace Pier** replaced it in 1899. Today it is decked in bunting and smells of pancakes, burgers and candyfloss. Thought by many to be the finest pier in existence, it is lent distinction by the Pavilion-style domes and filagree-work arches. Despite the souvenir shops, it still charms. Gone is the renowned Edwardian theatre, home of the Palace Pier Repertory Company, but other traditional entertainments are on offer: the ghost train, noisy slot machines and the helter skelter – as well as the possibility of

19 Below: *The Royal Crescent, completed in 1807, was the first of the many early-19th-century housing schemes in Brighton to be planned as a single architectural whole. The building was financed by J. B. Otto, a West Indian speculator; the architect is unknown. The houses stand on the cliff top facing the sea, all fronted with Brighton's distinctive black 'mathematical' tiles.*

20 Above: *Steine Gardens are dominated by the sparkling fountain, designed by A. H. Wilds. The lower base of its elaborate structure rests on the entwined figures of three dolphins, which also form part of the coat of arms of the Borough of Brighton.*

glimpsing the Isle of Wight from the top you have the added thrill of thinking you might spiral dizzily over the side and into the sea.

On the **beach** (**18**) you can crunch stones underfoot between striped deckchairs, spend an old penny in the National Museum of Penny Slot Machines under the arches (don't miss the gyrations of the 'Two Lovely Ladies'), or visit the Palace Pier Aquarium, which has a dolphinarium and a resident palmist, Madam Victoria.

Further along is the earlier **West Pier** (**15**). When it opened in 1866 it enraged Regency Square residents whose sea-view was spoilt. Known for its side-shows (including performing fleas and a cannon fired by the sun's rays), it was considered more 'select' than its rival and many of its visitors came from the nearby **Grand Hotel**. This opened in 1864, and was one of the first hotels to employ electric lights and lifts. When the **Metropole Hotel** opened in 1888, it was thought to clash with the Grand. Now its terracotta brick seems remarkably in tune, unlike the stark Brighton Centre nearby.

1893 brought **Volk's Railway**, the first regular electric train service in Britain. Christened 'Daddy Long Legs', it used to run between Brighton and Rottingdean along 24-foot-high stilts, to cope with tides. Cliff erosion forced that part of the line to close but the brown and yellow wagons still pass between Palace Pier and Black Rock Pool, near the Marina (April–September).

SS GREAT BRITAIN

Bristol

No other city in this book, except London, has succeeded in such worldly ways. Not primarily a cathedral city (like Canterbury) or a university town (like Oxford and Cambridge), Bristol grew to prominence as a port.

Bricgstow, the 'settlement by the bridge', was originally a hillock by the curves of the Rivers Avon and Frome, providing both safety and ready transport by water. The Saxons developed the secure anchorage and trading post into a fort. The Normans, realising the strategic value of the site, erected upon it a truly awesome castle, twice the size of Caernarfon – eventually razed by Cromwell during the Civil War.

Outside the Saxon fort rose the nucleus of Broad Street, Corn Street, Wine Street, Small Street and High Street. This medieval borough was itself enclosed by walls pierced by four main entrance gates, of which one survives – **St John's**, adorned with the sculptures of the Gaulish chiefs Brennus and Belinus, mythological founders of the town.

In the Middle Ages Cotswold wool and cloth were the major exports; later Bristol produced glass, pottery and porcelain. Imports included oil and fruit, silks and glass from Venice, spices from the East. The ships came up and moored at Bristol Bridge, a famous old structure, which was crammed with houses and a chapel. Under Henry II England acquired some of the finest wine-growing districts in France, generating the success of many importers; these later included Harveys (established 1796), who today maintain a fascinating **Wine Museum**.

Gradually a new class of prosperous merchants and craftsmen emerged, who banded together to form guilds that laid down rules of practice and codes of behaviour. The wealth amassed by certain traders rivalled, and sometimes exceeded, that of the nobility. Henry VII fined Bristol's merchants 'because their wives so finely dressed'. But the guilds funded schools, almshouses, hospitals and charities, and individual benefactors subsidised the creation of splendid churches.

With the discovery of America, ambitious voyages of exploration culminated in the colonisation of the New World. John Cabot reached North America from Bristol in 1497, believing he had found the mainland of Cathay (China). By the 17th century ships were sailing west from Bristol laden with refugees from religious persecution, nobility displaced by the Civil War, fortune hunters and simply men seeking a new life.

21 *Isambard Kingdom Brunel's SS* Great Britain, *the first large ship to be constructed of iron and fitted with a screw propellor, in the Bristol dry dock from which she was launched in 1843.*

As a result, trade between Britain and the New World blossomed. Tobacco from Barbados and Virginia was imported through Bristol, and sugar and rum from the West Indies. There would have been a veritable jungle of masts and rigging on the quaysides, while wharves and cellars were piled high with bales and hogsheads.

The atmosphere of this period can be recaptured in some of the famous inns near the docks. The Hole in the Wall, an 18th-century tavern overlooking the waterside, is claimed as the inspiration for the 'Spyglass' in Robert Louis Stevenson's *Treasure Island*, and the Llandoger Trow, a swaggering complex of bars converted from three timber-framed 17th-century houses, as the model for the 'Admiral Benbow'.

Victoria's reign brought railways, canals, Macadamised roads and the spectacular achievements of Isambard Kingdom Brunel (1806–59), who not only designed the **Clifton Suspension Bridge** (**22**) but planned the Great Western Railway, linking London to Bristol, and designed the **SS *Great Britain*** (**21**). As the terminus for the Great Western Railway, he erected at Temple Meads Station (1839) what is now the world's earliest surviving train shed, with a roof-span (unprecedented in its day) of 72 feet.

The industrial and naval importance of Bristol made it a bombing target during World War II, and many buildings were lost; but peace brought a determined recovery. One remarkable development was the construction of Concorde (1970) at Filton. Aerospace now figures among Bristol's major industries, with food, drink, tobacco, printing, packaging, chemicals, paints, plastics and the microchip.

While the castle was a gigantic statement of political and military strength, it was to be matched by an imposing expression of spiritual power. In 1140 an Augustinian abbey was founded on the hillside overlooking the walled medieval town. The Abbey Church, later much enlarged, now stands as a supreme achievement – **Bristol Cathedral** (**28**), of which Nikolaus Pevsner

22 *Brunel's masterpiece, the Clifton Suspension Bridge, spans the 250-foot chasm of the Avon Gorge, 245 feet above the high-water mark, between Clifton and Leigh Woods. It was opened in December 1863, four years after Brunel's death.*

OVERLEAF
A striking contrast in Broad Street:
23 (left) *The splendid elegance of Christ Church (1786–90), probably the work of William Paty.*
24 (right) *North-west of Christ Church, the bright art nouveau ceramic façade of Edward Everard's Printing House depicts Johann Gutenberg (c.1400–68), the first European to print with movable metal types; the Spirit of Literature; and William Morris, the English poet and craftsman who led the late-19th-century renaissance of fine printing.*

wrote, 'It proves incontrovertibly that English design surpassed that of all other countries during the first third of the C14.' The awe-inspiring nave was planned by Abbot Newland (1481–1515) to replace the Norman one, but the work was abandoned after the dissolution of the monasteries and not completed until 1868. The distinctive and beautiful lierne vaulting of the choir is early 14th century, with piers crowned by exuberant foliage capitals. This genius for enlivening detail is characteristic of the Cathedral. The misericord carvings in the choir abound with energy, as do the 13th-century carvings in the Elder Lady Chapel.

The original Norman chapter house, to the south, is decorated with zigzag and interlace, while the fine Norman arch on the south side of the cloister court and the archway of the **Abbey Gateway** are similarly remarkable for the dexterity and joyous mobility of their mouldings.

Another work of wonderful decoration is **St Mary Redcliffe**, whose soaring spire is a landmark for all south Bristol. Largely financed by the city's merchants, it was praised by Queen Elizabeth I as the 'fairest, goodliest and most famous parish church in England'. The inner north porch (*c.*1200) is a serene display of Early English craftsmanship; the hexagonal outer north porch is a masterpiece of Decorated work, surpassing all other examples of this rare form of approach to a church in its dazzling variety, density and delicacy of carved decoration. Inside, the nave's all-stone roof of ribbed vaulting branches out from over 1,200 gilded bosses.

Bristol seems to have been relatively hospitable to Nonconformists, who

GUTENBURG
MORRIS
EDWARD
EVERARD
National Westminster Court

produced rather more sober houses of worship. William Penn, founder of Pennsylvania, was a leading Bristol Quaker and the remains of the house of the Dominican Friars (now called the **Quakers' Friars**), bought in 1670, remained the chief meeting place of the Society of Friends for some three hundred years. In the 18th century the evangelising Wesley brothers, John and Charles, founded the Methodist sect. John's fire and ardour stirred hostility – he was barred from most parish churches – but eventually he acquired land in the Horsefair and erected the **New Room**, the first Methodist chapel (1748). Now surrounded by the Broadmead shopping centre, this still contains the double-decker pulpit from which Wesley preached.

Meanwhile private wealth showed itself in private dwellings. From early times timbered merchants' houses crowded close to the river, vantage points for close observation of the progress of their investments. **King Street**, laid out in 1663, still has a special old-world feel to it: a medley of red brick, stone, black-and-white timbering, cobbles and classical façades, with splashes of strong colour – ochre, red and blue. **Queen Square**, allegedly the largest in England after London's Lincoln's Inn Fields, is a more stately Bristolian composition. Its size makes the houses seem fairly modest, but leading Bristol merchants occupied these early-18th-century properties – hence the square was a target during the reform riots of 1831, when all of the north and most of the west sides were burnt down.

The city teems with dignified Georgian façades: Great George Street, off the major thoroughfare of **Park Street**, has a number of houses by William Paty – a particularly fine example is No. 7, now a museum known as **The Georgian House**. But the greatest concentration of such façades is found in what was formerly a separate village, **Clifton**, the best preserved area of Georgian and Regency squares, crescents and terraces outside Bath. Development began around 1775, encouraged by the boom of the Hotwell Spa.

25 Below: *Merchants Quay, part of the harmonious new housing development created along the waterfront of Bathurst Wharf. Bathurst Basin nearby is one of the three entrances to Bristol's Floating Harbour from the River Avon.*

26 Right: *The Granary (1871) is the last remaining warehouse building on Welsh Back, which was part of the Old Port where the Avon flowed. A spectacular example of the colourful variegated brick and stone style known as Bristol Byzantine, it is now a rock-music centre.*

BISTRO
GOOD FOOD
NOW BEING SERVED

27 Above: *The tomb erected in St Mary Redcliffe by its chief benefactor, William Canynges, for his wife Joanna, who died in 1467.*

28 Right: *The high altar and carved stone reredos in Bristol Cathedral were rebuilt by John Pearson in 1899, after the completion of the new nave.*

During the 1780s this was among the most visited spas in the kingdom, and Fanny Burney used it as the setting for her vivacious novel *Evelina* (1778). Like Bath it had its master of ceremonies and entertained guests with a chamber orchestra, dress balls and public breakfasts. The source of its celebrity was a spring of warm water which bubbled from the Avon mud, some of it bottled to be sold all over the world. But with the ending of the Napoleonic wars the resorts on the Continent were accessible once more and the spa declined.

Dowry Square was Hotwells' chief residential area, and here the Assembly Rooms were erected for balls, card-playing and evening parties. Above rises Cornwallis Crescent, begun in 1720; the architect was John Wood the Elder, who inaugurated the great neoclassical building developments at Bath. Beyond lies **Royal York Crescent**, perhaps the most impressive of Clifton's terraces, a calm and stately arc of Regency houses (1791–1820).

Commercial buildings, too, express Bristol's success. Corn Street was Bristol's major banking street during the 18th and 19th centuries. Here the **Corn Exchange** (**29**), 1743, dominates the pedestrianised area, flanked by the four equidistant Nails, dish-shaped brass tables on which merchants completed their transactions. The Victorians were more explicit: on Lloyds Bank (1854), inspired by Sansovino's Library in Venice, the commercial spirit in the frieze extolls the poetry of profit. The jauntiest building is Edward Everard's art nouveau Printing House (1901), in Broad Street, with a splendid façade of Doulton carrara (**24**). The colourful tiling depicts the Spirit of Literature presiding over ancient and modern printing, while Gutenberg and William Morris work at the press.

Since the end of the 1960s a major conservation programme has aimed at

ALL SAINTS LANE
CARWARDINE'S
Coffee

29 Left: *The Bristol Exchange (1741), the work of John Wood the Elder of Bath. Two of the four Nails on which merchants formerly transacted their business can be seen here in front of the imposing Palladian façade. The pedestrianisation of this part of Corn Street has completed its transformation from the hub of commerce to a leisurely piazza-like area.*

30 Above: *Charlotte Street, seen here through the trees at the foot of Brandon Hill, is typical of Bristol's many 18th-century streets and squares.*

restoring buildings of special historical and architectural interest. Late Georgian and early Victorian warehouses around St Augustine's Reach have been refurbished and transformed into the **Watershed Media Centre** and the **Arnolfini Gallery**. In the same spirit the **Bristol Industrial Museum** was opened in 1978 and contains, among other artefacts, the world's oldest steam-driven car (1875), Bristol cars of the 1940s, Bristol aero-engines, and a mock-up of the nose section of Concorde. Bristol's pioneering role in nautical history is wonderfully expressed in a gallery which traces the story of the city docks and re-creates a 19th-century marine workshop.

The **Maritime Heritage Centre** possesses a unique collection of ship-models, marine architects' drawings, paintings, prints and nautical instruments, as well as a full-size copy of the BD6, Brunel's famous dredger. The star attraction is Brunel's SS *Great Britain.* This wrought-iron ship, the first to be fitted with a screw propeller, was launched in the presence of Prince Albert in 1843. After several voyages to North America and Australia, she was wrecked on the Falkland Islands. In 1970 she was towed back to Bristol and a programme of restoration began.

On the waterfront of St Augustine's Reach, between the Watershed and the Arnolfini, is, appropriately, the statue of Neptune cast by the local founder John Randell (1723), a reminder of the historical bond between Bristol and the sea.

Cambridge

Most people know of Cambridge because of the annual boat race when the University challenges that other great seat of learning, Oxford. But day-trippers coming to take snaps of King's Chapel and to try out their own nautical skills punting on the river discover a thriving city of bookshops, tea-shops and historic pubs. Ringing the centre are green open spaces: Christ's Pieces, Parker's Piece, Jesus Green and Midsummer Common. The Fellows' Garden of Clare College (**43**) and the **Backs** (**36**), landscaped in the 18th century between the riverside colleges and the water, complete the circle.

The River Cam drew settlers here as early as Neolithic times (you can examine pre-Roman relics in the **Museum of Archaeology and Anthropology** on Sidgwick Avenue). By AD43 the Romans had bridged the river, setting up a fortified camp on its northern bank. When they departed Cambridge fell in turn to Danes, Vikings and Saxons. The last built churches on the formerly prosperous south bank and one on the north bank, **St Peter's**, Castle Hill, which occupies the site of a Roman temple of Diana. Saxon architecture is still visible at **St Bene't's**, whose tower (1025) is the oldest building in Cambridgeshire. Linked to Corpus Christi College by a gallery, St Bene't's served as college chapel until the 16th century.

In the Middle Ages Cambridge prospered. On the steep mound of Castle Hill stood a castle built by William the Conqueror. A more domestic building of this period survives in St John's College grounds: Dunningstede, now named '**School of Pythagoras**', rebuilt in the late 12th century by the first elected Mayor. Of the religious houses, the **Round Church** endures (largely restored in the 19th century).

The history of the University starts in 1209, when scholars fled here from riots in Oxford. The rift between 'town and gown' is also traced back to this time, for the refugees were not welcomed by the tradesmen of Cambridge. The scholars brought money, which upset the system of bartering, and soon there were disagreements over what the students should be charged for provisions. Squabbles flared into fights and after one incident in 1261, 16 townsmen were hanged. But the University won royal backing. In the 14th century the King allowed the University to price food and drink, compelling the Mayor and town bailiffs, when they took office, to swear to maintain University privileges. This unpopular measure lasted until 1856.

In the Middle Ages the University consisted solely of a guild of teachers which owned the **Old Schools**, dating from 1350 but now much altered. The faculties of divinity, law and the arts were housed here, together with the library. Since the 18th-century Copyright Acts the library has received a copy of every book published in Great Britain. The growing collection was rehoused across the river in 1934. Old Schools became the home of the law faculty, while the University State Rooms occupy the rest of the quadrangle.

31 *Graduates in formal academic dress outside the Senate House, where degrees are conferred.*

32 Left: *Christ's College main gate: above is the coat of arms of Lady Margaret Beaufort. The yales supporting the shield are mythical beasts, able to rotate their horns at will.*

33 Above: *The Old Court of Corpus Christi College, the best surviving example in Cambridge of an early medieval college court (1352–78), with late-15th-century buttresses.*

Few medieval students lasted the seven-year course. Grammar, rhetoric and logic (the *trivium*) formed the syllabus of the Bachelor of Arts degree; some graduates then continued to complete the *quadrivium* (arithmetic, music, astronomy and geography) to win the degree of Master of Arts. Today students practise rhetoric in the **Union Society**, which has its own buildings behind the Round Church: debates are staged involving eminent guest speakers.

The modern undergraduate course at Cambridge is called a 'Tripos' after the three-legged stools used in medieval examinations. Exam results are pinned up outside the 18th-century **Senate House**, and it is here that graduands in formal academic dress (a hood trimmed with white rabbit-fur) accept their degrees (**31**). Medieval degrees, however, were conferred in the University Church of **Great St Mary's**. Climb to the top of the tower and all Cambridge spreads before you. The quarter-hour chimes of the clock, copied in 1859 for Big Ben, have been adopted throughout the world under the name of 'Westminster Chimes'.

Since the 13th century Cambridge scholars have lived and studied in individual communities – at first halls of residence, now colleges. The oldest college, **Peterhouse**, has stood on its present site since 1284. Refashioned over the centuries, its 15th-century First Court is adorned with classical 18th-century façades. The Church of St Peter's-without-Trumpington-Gate, now known as Little St Mary's, is linked to Peterhouse by a gallery but was replaced as college chapel in the 17th century by an English Baroque addition

to the main court. This new chapel suffered at the hands of Puritan soldiers. Hidden until the Restoration, its great east window – made to a Rubens design – miraculously survived.

Clare College was founded 14 years after Peterhouse. But it only got its present name in 1338 when, after a period of decline, it was re-established by Edward I's granddaughter Lady Elizabeth de Clare, who planned to provide education for poor boys. Most of Clare's elegant buildings are 17th century, as is Thomas Grumbold's stone bridge, one of the prettiest crossing the Cam. Clare is also distinguished by its intricate 18th-century wrought-iron entrance gates, and the beautiful Fellows' Garden (**43**) tucked away on the other side of the water.

Gonville and Caius was founded once in 1348 and again in 1557. Edmund Gonville died shortly after purchasing the site. In 1557 Dr John Caius (pronounced 'keys'), as Master, procured more land and designed a new court to be named after him. In his will, Caius (who instigated the college's reputation for medical study) left instructions for keeping the buildings clean. His designs included the three gates which mark the steps in a student's career: Humility, Virtue and finally Honour, the charmingly festive gate to Senate House Passage, through which undergraduates passed to Old Schools to sit their exams.

One of the most appealing of the smaller colleges is **Trinity Hall**. Intended by its patron, the Bishop of Norwich, to encourage scholars of canon law, for over six hundred years the college has had a reputation for producing legal luminaries. You get an idea of what the 14th-century main court was once like by walking through B staircase passage; the wall immediately behind retains

34 Above: *Trinity Hall: the herbaceous border outside the Tudor Library.*

35 Right: *Jesus College: the chapel, once the church of St Radegund's Convent (founded in the early 12th century); the upper part of the tower is a 15th-century addition.*

some medieval masonry and small windows. The chapel, Cambridge's tiniest and the earliest designed for college use, is 18th century in appearance. The library, however, still flaunts its Elizabethan brickwork. On the upper floor books remain chained to their Jacobean bookcases – a pre-electronic security device. Pleasant gardens (**34**) lead down to the riverside terrace, and beyond the Master's Lodge extends the Fellows' Garden, 'the prettiest corner in the world' according to the novelist Henry James.

Trinity Hall counts among its graduates Viscount Fitzwilliam, who, in the 19th century, left the University his substantial art collection together with £100,000 to build the **Fitzwilliam Museum**. In 1967 H.S. Ede did much the same, bequeathing to the University his house, **Kettle's Yard**, and his impressive collection of 20th-century art.

Two Cambridge guilds were responsible for the first college to be centrally located. **Corpus Christi** was founded in 1352 by the Guilds of Corpus Christi and of the Blessed Virgin Mary. It was known until the last century as Bene't College, and for many years the townsfolk considered it their own. Its Old Court (**33**) is the best surviving example of a medieval college quadrangle. Here the ghost of Dr Butts has been sighted. Master of the College 1626–32, he hanged himself shortly before he was due to give the University sermon. Here too resided Christopher Marlowe, the Elizabethan dramatist whose portrait (now hanging in the hall) was discovered in the 20th century behind wainscotting in the college.

In the mid-14th century the University gave Mary de St Pol, Countess of Pembroke, a patch of land to build **Pembroke College**. Old Court has a

King's College:
36 (below) *A view across the Backs in early spring; to the right of the chapel is Gibbs' Fellows' Building and to the left is Clare College Old Court.*
37 (right) *The east end of the Chapel. The windows, designed by Flemish glaziers, are an especially valuable survival in England, which lost most of its early stained glass during 16th- and 17th-century religious upheavals.*

14th-century gateway topped by 17th-century oriel windows which flank the college coat of arms carved in stone. The present chapel is the first completed work of Sir Christopher Wren, whose uncle, Bishop of Ely and fellow of Pembroke, bore the expense. Other Pembroke men include the church reformer Nicholas Ridley, the poets Thomas Gray and Christopher Smart, and the politician William Pitt, who matriculated in 1773, aged 15, and ten years later was Prime Minister.

God's House became **Christ's College** (**32**) in 1505, when Lady Margaret Beaufort set about enlarging the college, which had been founded in 1439 to train schoolmasters. Its statutes reveal a stern mistress: for instance, only Latin could be spoken, misbehaving students were fined (those under 21 years old were beaten), and drinking, trading, hunting and gambling were prohibited. The Fellows' Building, begun in 1640, is attributed to Inigo Jones. Beyond stretches the Fellows' Garden, complete with 18th-century bathing pool and garden house. The mulberry tree is possibly one of three hundred bought in 1608. It is traditionally associated with Milton, who, as a student (1625–32), had such a delicate appearance that he was dubbed 'the lady of Christ's'. Two of his early poems composed here concern a local carter, Thomas Hobson, whose custom of making clients accept the horse nearest the stable door supposedly originated the phrase 'Hobson's Choice'.

King's College is internationally famous, especially for its chapel (**37**), the subject of paintings by Turner and Canaletto and of poems by Wordsworth and Betjeman. From here Christmas Eve carols are broadcast yearly to a worldwide audience. The chapel is all that was realised of Henry VI's scheme for a new college. The foundation stone was laid in 1446 but building ceased in 1461 with Henry's deposition. Outside at the western end you can see where the original white limestone stops about 5 feet above ground level. Successive kings continued the work. Henry VII commissioned the fan vaulting; Henry VIII financed the organ screen and the stained-glass windows, which depict Old and New Testament scenes. The chapel was finished 99 years after its conception, while the rest of Great Court was not completed until three hundred years later. In the 19th century King's students lost the enviable right to claim a degree without sitting examinations. The novelist E.M. Forster, the economist Maynard Keynes and the poet Rupert Brooke were all King's men.

Along the river you find **Queens'**, once St Bernard's College. Within a year of its foundation (1446) Henry VI's queen, Margaret of Anjou, renamed the college. When the royal couple were deposed, the new queen, Elizabeth, granted it statutes and finished the building. The ladies, though enemies, are both remembered as benefactresses. The mellow red-brick First Court gives a good impression of a late-medieval college. The picturesque timber and plaster gallery of the President's Lodge (**38**) – Queens' has a President rather than a Master – connects First Court to the river buildings. On three sides of the court the medieval cloister (Cambridge's single example) creates an ideal setting for summer productions of Shakespeare's plays. Erasmus' Tower in the south-west corner of Old Court is named after the humanist scholar who resided at Queens' from 1511 to 1514. The mathematical bridge is a 20th-century copy of the 1749 original.

38 *Queens' College: the President's Lodge, a beautiful example of early-16th-century domestic architecture.*

The name and crest (a wheel) of **St Catharine's College** derive from the mythical patroness of learning, whose sanctity shattered the wheel she was to be martyred upon. In 1473 the original intake consisted of priests studying theology and philosophy (medicine and law were forbidden). Most of the buildings date from the 17th century. The University's youngest ever undergraduate entered St Catharine's at this time too: he was nine years old.

St John's College, like Christ's, was one of Lady Margaret Beaufort's projects. She died before the foundation in 1511 and it was her friend the Bishop of Rochester who brought the college into being. First Court incorporated the chapel of the 13th-century Hospital of St John, originally on this site. The beautiful gatehouse bears Lady Margaret's coat of arms above the entrance. For a long time the college was the University's largest. Another aristocratic lady – Mary, Countess of Shrewsbury – paid for Second Court and her statue poses above the tower gateway at the west end of the court. Within this plain Elizabethan brickwork building runs the spectacular panelled Long Gallery. Its 90-foot-long plaster ceiling dates from 1600.

Passing over the early-18th-century bridge at the back of St John's, you can imagine the poet Wordsworth doing the same, for as an undergraduate he often wandered here. In 1831 the huge New Building was erected on the other side of the river. Crowned with a Gothic cupola (nicknamed the Wedding Cake) it is attached to Third Court by the Bridge of Sighs (**39**).

How different is **Jesus College** with open courts set in spacious grounds, its lofty chapel (**35**) and some of its other buildings originally part of the 12th-century Priory of St Radegund. John Alcock, Bishop of Ely, founded Jesus in 1496. His rebus (punning badge), a cockerel on a globe, is dotted all over the college. Although the old chapter house of the priory had been demolished, in the 19th century its beautiful arcaded 13th-century entrance was uncovered behind a wall of Cloister Court, which is itself 16th century. In the 19th century too the chapel was refurbished with stained glass by Sir Edward Burne-Jones and paintings on the nave ceiling by his fellow Pre-Raphaelite William Morris. Notable graduates of Jesus include the reforming bishop Thomas Cranmer, the novelist Laurence Sterne, the poet Samuel Taylor Coleridge, the scientist Jacob Bronowski and, more recently, Prince Edward.

Magdalene College (pronounced 'maudlin') is the one ancient college on the north bank. Incorporating buildings of a Benedictine monks' hostel, it was also known as Buckingham College because of endowments left by the Dukes of Buckingham in the late 15th century. The present college was founded in 1542 by Thomas, Lord Audley, Lord Chancellor of England, whose heirs still appoint the Master. The fine red-brick court was erected in the 15th and 16th centuries. The 17th-century Pepys Building houses the library that the diarist Samuel Pepys left to his old college, still contained in the 12 red oak bookcases he had made for it in 1666. Magdalene Street is mostly college property. Once a slum notorious for its brothels, it now consists of picturesque shops.

Wealth, intellectual distinction and architectural splendour characterise **Trinity College** (**40**). In 1546 Henry VIII united two existing colleges to rival Christ Church in Oxford, which had been established by Wolsey, his discredited Chancellor. The Great Gate through which you enter from Trinity Street and the clock tower in Great Court, bearing a statue of Edward III, both date from this time. A 16th-century master, Thomas Nevile, cleared Great Court of buildings, moved the clock tower to its present position and raised a second tower with a statue of Elizabeth I. He also built the hall (**42**) – the largest in Cambridge – and the fountain, to provide college members with

39 *St John's College: the Bridge of Sighs spans the River Cam, linking the college's 17th-century Third Court with the New Building (1831) on the west bank. It resembles the Bridge of Sighs in Venice only in being a covered bridge.*

drinking water. Beyond the hall Nevile constructed a court (**41**), now named after him, and now closed off from the river by Wren's magnificent library, which can sometimes be visited. Wren himself designed the library stools and the revolving reading tables; the lavish limewood carvings decorating the bookcases are the work of Grinling Gibbons.

A number of famous poets studied at Trinity: they include Herbert, Marvell, Dryden, Byron and Tennyson, whose *In Memorian* recalls the avenue of limes and James Essex's 18th-century bridge onto the Backs. In the ante-chapel are memorials to other illustrious graduates, including the scientist Sir Isaac Newton, the philosopher Bertrand Russell, and Sir Francis Bacon, Lord Chancellor to James I. Prince Charles was a student at Trinity between 1967 and 1970.

Emmanuel College occupies the site of a religious house dissolved by Henry VIII in 1538, which Sir Walter Mildmay, Chancellor of the Exchequer to Elizabeth I, acquired in 1583 as a place to prepare men for Church careers. It became a principal centre of Protestant theology, and suffered during the High-Church revival under Charles I. Emigrants to the New World at this time included Emmanuel graduates such as John Harvard, who gave his name to the American university. Original monastic buildings were assimilated into the fabric of the college, but the new chapel was designed by Wren; sculptured garlands and festoons lend it a festive appearance. Floodlit at night, the façade appears like a backdrop for a 17th-century masque. In the grounds the lake where Fellows bathed has been given over to ducks.

Constructed on the site of a 13th-century friary, **Sidney Sussex College** was established by the will of Lady Frances Sidney, Countess of Sussex. Most

40 Below: *The dining hall and central fountain in Trinity Great Court, laid out at the end of the 16th century by Thomas Nevile, master of the college. To the right of the hall is the Senior Combination Room.*

41 Above: *Nevile's Court, Trinity College. Initially open to the river, it was enclosed by the addition of a new library (1676–95), designed by Sir Christopher Wren, and visible here through the arches of the elegant semi-classical cloister.*

of the 16th-century brick buildings survive but were stuccoed in the 19th century. In 1616 Oliver Cromwell entered the college (he subsequently became MP for Cambridge), but Sidney Sussex never showed Parliamentarian sympathies; in fact it sent £100 to the King during the Civil War and the Master was imprisoned for refusing to donate to Parliamentary funds. In 1960 Cromwell's severed head was buried secretly in the chapel. Whenever the monarch is toasted in hall curtains are drawn across the Protector's portrait which hangs there.

In 1717 Sir George Downing made provision in his will for what was to be the last of the older colleges. Unfortunately Lady Downing entered into prolonged litigation to keep hold of his cash and so **Downing College** was not established until 1800. In 1882 a new college run on Church of England principles, **Selwyn College**, was conceived.

By this time the first women's college had been established – **Girton College**, founded in 1869 and located 3 miles out of town at a safe distance from male undergraduates. **Newnham College**, also for women, followed in 1871. In 1890 Philippa Fawcett caused a sensation by scoring the highest marks in the mathematical tripos. Even so, women were not awarded degrees. Despite the fact that so many women had instigated colleges, Cambridge remained misogynistic. In 1897 a ballot was held to decide whether women should be admitted to degrees, and trainloads of voters came from London to veto the idea. An effigy of a female student in bloomers on a bicycle was dangled from a shop window, while male graduates pelted flour at dons

SEMPER EADEM

42 Left: *Trinity College dining hall: a view of the interior showing the notable double hammer-beam ceiling. This hall was closely modelled on the hall of Middle Temple, London. The founder's portrait hangs above high table.*

43 Above: *Clare College Fellows' Garden: one of the most beautiful of many such gardens in the older colleges.*

waiting to vote. Only in 1947 were women allowed to receive degrees.

Among Cambridge's more recently established colleges are **Churchill College** (1960), a national monument to the great statesman Sir Winston Churchill, and **Fitzwilliam College** (1964), designed by architect Sir Denys Lasdun. **New Hall**, for women, opened in 1954. By 1970 the University intake of women still only represented 12 per cent of the total but two years later King's, Clare and Churchill began to alter the balance by being the first colleges to become co-residential; now all the colleges admit women. And the founding of colleges goes on. **Darwin College**, **Wolfson College** and **Clare Hall**, mainly for graduates, have all been founded since World War II. The last undergraduate college to be opened was **Robinson** (named after its local millionaire benefactor), which welcomed its first students in 1980.

HIGH ST.
Boots
PARADE
Boots
Dispensing Chemists

Canterbury

Canterbury might have been simply a prosperous market town. It lies within what has been historically the richest part of Kent, the Garden of England; and its produce has always been easily transportable to London and to the Continent. But that convenient situation also put the city directly in the way of military and political currents. It was the pre-Conquest capital of Kent; and in 1066 William passed through Canterbury as he advanced from Dover to London. Here the Normans built imposing city walls and a very large castle – the name is retained in the Dane John (= Norman 'donjon') Gardens.

But the history of Canterbury is bound up with religion. The city's greatness developed out of the confrontation between two kings and two archbishops, in one case a story of co-operation, in the other of collision; from both the see of Canterbury emerged triumphantly strengthened in unanticipated ways.

Canterbury – Saxon Cantwarbyrig – was already the major city of the Kingdom of Kent, ruled by the pagan King Ethelbert, when Pope Gregory the Great sent Augustine, Prior of the monastery of St Andrew in Rome, to convert England to Christianity. (A Bible believed to have been given by Pope Gregory to St Augustine is in the library of Corpus Christi College, Cambridge.) Apparently Gregory intended that English Christians be governed from two sees, at London and York. Augustine came to Canterbury first, and here on Whitsunday in 597 King Ethelbert was baptised. Canterbury may originally have been only a stopping-point for Augustine, and his church was essentially that of the Kingdom of Kent. But the strong support of the Kentish reign, and the difficulties which impeded the further spread of Christianity, helped to confirm Canterbury as the Christian focus it has remained. Since the 14th century the Archbishop of Canterbury has been Primate of all England, giving the office a power even over kings.

With the King's support Augustine first established a monastery (later named after him), of which some ruins still remain (**45**). It came to be a great centre of learning, and a great landholder. St Augustine was buried there himself, as were King Ethelbert and his queen. The Queen had worshipped at **St Martin's**, which may date from Roman times and is today almost certainly the oldest church in England: it has been in continuous use at least since the reign of Ethelbert. Nearby was another building, possibly the remains of a still earlier church, and here Augustine began to build his **Cathedral** in 602. Successive rebuildings have obliterated the Saxon cathedral, first after the Conquest when William's appointee, Lanfranc, vigorously set about repairing what the Danes and fire had destroyed. His building was beautifully constructed of stone brought from Caen in Normandy; the best remains of it can be seen in the present **crypt**. His north-west tower stood until the 19th century, when it was replaced to harmonise with the west front.

Under Lanfranc the Priory became the largest monastic foundation in the

44 *A view down St Margaret's Street through the Christ Church Gate (1517) to the Cathedral beyond.*

country. Regal and religious co-operation had produced a powerful Christian centre. But confrontation was to occur in the next century. Thomas Becket (1118–70), an able administrator, rose to the staff of Archbishop Theobald, and in 1154 on the succession of Henry II was recommended by the Archbishop as Chancellor. Relations between King and Chancellor were close, and when Theobald died in 1161 Thomas was made Archbishop of Canterbury as well. But he displeased the King by resigning as Chancellor, and his insistence on the judicial and financial rights of the Church now brought them into conflict.

In 1164 Thomas went into exile in France, excommunicating his enemies while offering his resignation to the Pope. A brief reconciliation with the King lasted only a few weeks: Thomas returned to Canterbury in December 1170 to popular acclaim but with premonitions of his martyrdom. When he was again accused before Henry in Normandy, the King burst forth with his famous cry, 'Who will rid me of this turbulent priest?' Four knights, supplying his meaning, crossed over to England and confronted Thomas with charges of treason. Anxious monks took their bishop for safety to the Cathedral, where the knights pursued him and slew him during vespers.

This political act had enormous religious consequences. In a moment the character of Canterbury changed forever. Within a few days miracles began to occur; and in 1173 Becket was canonised by Pope Alexander III. Henry came to do penance. Just six weeks later a fire destroyed the choir. Work began at once on the east end of the Cathedral, now for the construction of a shrine to St Thomas. Canterbury became a pilgrim city, especially after 1220 when King

45 Above: *The ruins of St Augustine's Abbey.*

46 Right: *Canterbury Cathedral seen from the north, across the site of the main monastic buildings of the 11th and 12th centuries.*

OVERLEAF

47 Left: *The Old Weavers' House (1507), in St Peter's Street.*

48 Right: *The unique Norman staircase in the Green Court (c.1153) of the former Priory leads to the heavily rebuilt remnant of the North Hall, now King's School library.*

come
to see
how
wool is
spun

Canterbury Cathedral:
49 (left) *The tomb of Edward, the Black Prince (d.1376), eldest son of Edward III, on the south side of Trinity Chapel. Above the effigy hangs a painted canopy and, above that, replicas of the Prince's surcoat, helmet and gauntlets. According to the chronicler Froissart, he earned his sobriquet by his ferocity – not because he wore a black suit of armour.*
50 (right) *The choir was rebuilt by William of Sens, a pioneer of the Gothic style, after a fire in 1174. The aisle pillars, taller and slimmer than in earlier Norman churches, support black Purbeck marble shafts, and their carving is reflected in the capitals of the columns below the clerestory, from which the roof vaults spring. Trinity Chapel and the Corona, the circular chamber at the easternmost end which creates an effect of depth and distance, were completed after the Frenchman's death.*

Henry III headed the procession in which the saint's body was translated to its magnificently jewelled shrine in **Trinity Chapel**. The Cathedral gained overwhelming prestige in the community of Christians everywhere as worshippers arrived from all over Britain and Europe; an amusing mixture of English pilgrims travelling to the shrine was created by Chaucer in his *Canterbury Tales*. The shrine survived until 1538, when Henry VIII had it stripped of its treasures and destroyed.

Pilgrimage provided continuing revenue for both the Cathedral and the city throughout the Middle Ages. In addition both Cathedral and Priory had acquired agricultural lands in Kent, whose excellently managed production of cereals, dairy products and wool made the area one of the most prosperous parts of England. Other lands provided regular income from rents.

It was this steady flow of funds to the church that made its physical enrichment possible. Lafranc's Norman nave was demolished in 1377, the glorious new Perpendicular one finished in 1405. The ground-plan was dictated by the Norman original, but not the height – it is wonderfully spacious and airy, full of light from the large aisle and clerestory windows. Within a few years the nave was embellished by the south porch (1418), which probably commemorates the victory at Agincourt in 1415. At the crossing was erected the great eye-catching crossing tower, Bell Harry, begun 1494. Originally it was intended to rise to only half its present height, and would have been much less successful in pulling together the rather rambling whole of the cathedral.

Fortunately a second tall story was added, of brick faced with Caen stone.

Of all the treasures within the Cathedral the most important is the complex beyond the altar: everything to the east of the choir was erected in honour of St Thomas. The significance of the shrine is announced by the levels which rise to it: steps lead from the nave to the choir (**50**), from the choir to the presbytery and altar, from them to Trinity Chapel and the **Corona** (**51**). This is how the pilgrims ascended to the shrine for over three hundred years, and it is moving to see that the steps to the chapel are worn by their knees. In the chapel are remains of the wonderful pavement which surrounded the shrine, a geometrical pattern flanked by 36 roundels of virtues and vices, the months of the year and signs of the zodiac. In the chapel ambulatory a remarkable quantity of late-12th-century glass survives, including illustrations of the life, death and posthumous miracles of St Thomas, painted within a decade after his death. Almost as old is 'St Augustine's Chair', probably of the 13th century, on which each successive archbishop is enthroned.

Also in Trinity Chapel, in prudent proximity to the shrine, stands the tomb of Henry IV (1367–1413) and his queen, Joan of Navarre (d.1437), with lavish alabaster effigies. Here too is one of the most splendid memorials in England, of Edward the Black Prince (1330–76), eldest son of Edward III, bearing the original copper gilt effigy (**49**). Replicas of the armour borne at his funeral include his helmet and shield.

The Cathedral was badly damaged in 1642 when Cromwellian troopers attacked the altar and the font, destroyed much of the furniture, smashed glass, and pulled away lead and brass. But wonderful examples of medieval decoration have survived. There are wall-paintings of the 12th century in St Gabriel's Chapel in the crypt, where the apse has an entire sequence of *c.*1130, including scenes of the Annunciation and Nativity; and in St Anselm's Chapel, a contemporary painting of St Paul and the viper on Malta. More plentiful and striking is the stained glass: Canterbury has the finest 12th- and 13th-century glass in the country. Aside from the Miracle windows of Trinity Chapel, the 'Theological' windows of the north choir aisle are notable, with Old Testament scenes foreshadowing New Testament ones.

The Norman crypt is the earliest and largest in England, with the original columns and elaborately carved figures on the capitals. The eastern chapel under Trinity Chapel and the Corona was the first burial site of St Thomas.

Many buildings accumulated around the cathedral. Immediately adjacent is the **Great Cloister** (1397–1414), mainly Perpendicular in style but with some fine Norman work and beautiful Early English arcading in the north walk. The painted bosses of the lierne vaulting, which include over eight hundred shields, are superb. The roomy 14th-century **chapter house** was the setting for the first performance of T.S. Eliot's *Murder in the Cathedral* in 1935.

While the Cathedral survived, the Priory suffered much from the dissolution of the monasteries. A striking remnant is the 12th-century exterior Norman staircase in the Green Court, still in use. Some of the Priory was incorporated in **King's School** (**48**), the grammar school which was installed here by Henry VIII (its most famous student was Christopher Marlowe).

Canterbury was heavily bombed in 1942, when about a third of the old city was destroyed. But some of the surviving buildings and narrow lanes suggest the medieval town. **Westgate** still stands, a fine fortified gate through which kings and pilgrims made their way into the city. The pilgrims stayed at the

51 *The early-13th-century windows in the Corona are fine examples of the best of the Cathedral's glass. Arranged around the central panels illustrating the principal events from Good Friday to Pentecost are prophetic scenes from the Old Testament.*

Hospital of St Thomas the Martyr or **Eastbridge Hospital**, built about 1175 to accommodate them.

The town also has traces of the houses established by religious orders. **Greyfriars** is the remains of the first Franciscan settlement in England; and **Blackfriars**, on the Stour, was founded by Dominicans *c.*1240. Also on the Stour is the **Old Weavers' House** (**47**), a fine timber-framed building of 1507. It takes its name from Flemish and Huguenot weavers who settled in Canterbury in the 16th and 17th centuries. Their descendants still maintain a special place of worship in the Black Prince's Chantry in the Cathedral crypt.

London

The monuments of nearly two thousand years' history attract many millions of visitors to London each year, but the city's vast scale and complex layout can be bewildering. Often London seems to take pleasure in hiding its attractions and presenting visitors with a blank face. A quick tour of the major sights may be uninspiring – Buckingham Palace is closed and aloof, Trafalgar Sqare a nightmare of traffic and even St Paul's seems casually hidden away. What is the best way to unlock all that London has to offer?

Part of the problem is that London is largely unplanned. The city's Edwardian heyday as capital of a world empire saw some attempts to create imperial urban set-pieces: Kingsway and the Aldwych, for instance, or Admiralty Arch, linking the Mall with Trafalgar Square. But London remains intriguingly – and sometimes infuriatingly – informal. There is no plan that the visitor can instantly recognise – no Parisian boulevards and nothing like Vienna's Ring or Manhattan's avenues. But two important facts are soon obvious: the size of the city, and its ancient division between east and west, between commerce and power, between merchant and court, between work and pleasure.

To appreciate London's size some height is needed. The top of any tall building will do, but the most pleasurable and enlightening way to spend a first fine morning in London is to avoid buildings altogether and take a tube or bus to **Regent's Park**. There, just north of the zoo, on the other side of a canal, is Primrose Hill. Although it is only 206 feet high, the view from the top is astonishing. To the south all London lies before you; on a clear day you can see beyond it to the hills of Surrey and Kent. There is a plan indicating all the major landmarks; amongst them the great dome of St Paul's Cathedral to the east and the towers of the Houses of Parliament to the west. But the most impressive feature is the endless sea of anonymous buildings that extends in all directions.

52 *The White Tower, the central keep of the Tower of London, was built between 1077 and 1097 under the direction of Gundulf, Bishop of Rochester. It is one of the finest examples of Norman military architecture in the country. Constructed of stone specially imported from France, its walls are 12 feet thick at the base. The windows were remodelled by Wren early in the 18th century.*

To experience the city's historic division, begin with a place that must be high on every visitor's agenda, the **Tower of London** (**52**). The grim fortress founded by William the Conqueror, to control the capital of the newly subjugated English, has been much enlarged since Norman times. Formerly a prison, where many great figures have been condemned to live and some to die (Sir Walter Ralegh and Henry VIII's wife Anne Boleyn among them), it is still a barracks, whose soldiers protect the Crown Jewels. After visiting the Tower and having admired the ravens and Beefeaters (**61**) who live there, go down to the **River Thames** and take a boat to Westminster. It is not a long journey – about three-quarters of an hour – and many important features of London will become apparent.

The Thames is the reason for London's existence. 'London' may be a Celtic name (Llyn-din, meaning river place), but evidence of settlements before the

Romans conquered the island in AD43 has only very recently been discovered and is not yet fully understood. The Romans bridged the Thames here, choosing a spot just above the then tidal limit, with firm land both north and south that would be good for building. Soon the town was not just a military outpost but a trading and financial centre, and shortly after AD60 London was created capital of the new Roman province of Britannia. There are few reminders of London's Roman past on her streets today, but extensive archaeological excavations have uncovered many artefacts, some of which can be seen in the **Museum of London** in the Barbican.

The Roman city covered the area known today as 'the City' – a square mile that is the heart of the country's financial life. For many centuries the City *was* London; there was a much smaller medieval settlement south of the river, with its own cathedral at Southwark (**53**), but the London that visitors want to see is almost exclusively north of the Thames. This is evident on the boat journey – to the north (on your right as you approach Westminster) the buildings are mostly quite grand; to the south only offices, wharves and warehouses before the modern buildings of the **South Bank** arts complex around Waterloo Bridge. Behind you to the east, beyond the Gothic towers and the drawbridge of **Tower Bridge** (built 1886–94), extend London's old docklands, now being energetically developed with offices for the ever-expanding workings of the City and homes for the affluent executives. The docks themselves have moved much farther down river, outside London altogether.

Look to the west, ahead of you. This has been London's main direction of growth. During the 11th century, six hundred years after the Romans had left Britain, the kings moved their residence from Winchester to Westminster, about a mile upstream of London. Shortly afterwards, Edward the Confessor began to rebuild the abbey next door to the new palace, for he intended to be buried there. Ever since then **Westminster** has been the centre of England's political life. The arrival of the royal palace and the rebuilding of the abbey gave London two centres: the City, the old London, the centre of trade, huddled around old St Paul's Cathedral, and the West End, the seat of government and the most fashionable residential area, with **Westminster Abbey** as *its* ecclesiastical centrepiece; the two centres are linked by a long riverside street, the Strand.

The boat berths at Westminster Bridge, a minute's walk from Parliament Square. To the south are the **Houses of Parliament** (**55**), part of the Palace of Westminster; to the west is Westminster Abbey; and to the east is Whitehall, lined with government offices, which leads to **Trafalgar Square**.

Scarcely anything remains of Edward the Confessor's abbey and palace. In 1245 Henry III demolished the choir of the old abbey, and began a great Gothic church to rival those being built in France; it was intended to be a shrine to Edward the Confessor, who had been canonised in 1161, and to serve as a coronation church and a home for the regalia. The regalia are now at the Tower, but in every other way the Abbey continues to serve Henry's purposes: it still houses the Confessor's shrine and every English monarch since William the Conqueror has been anointed here (with the exception of Edward V, who was murdered before he could be crowned, and Edward VIII, who abdicated before his coronation).

The building's tall and slimly proportioned interior is thrillingly beautiful,

53 *Southwark Cathedral: the retrochoir, the earliest part of the present cathedral, dates from the early 13th century. This view shows the beautiful blind arcading behind the high altar.*

RICHARD I
CŒUR DE LION
1189 – 1199

54 Left: *Richard Coeur de Lion, the crusader king (by Marochetti, 1860), outside the Houses of Parliament in Old Palace Yard. In 1606 this was the scene of the execution of Guy Fawkes, who had tried to blow up Parliament.*

55 Above: *The Houses of Parliament from Victoria Tower Gardens. The Victoria Tower at the left (336 feet), used to store archives, contains the original copy of every Act passed by 'the mother of Parliaments' since 1497.*

but a great effort has to be made to imagine it as it looked before it became the nation's Valhalla, for it is now a bewildering warehouse of monuments of all ages and every type. These are often extraordinarily interesting themselves. Pride of place must go to the great medieval royal tombs: in the Confessor's Chapel are buried Henry III, Edward I and Eleanor of Castile, Edward III and Philippa of Hainault, Richard II and Anne of Bohemia. Henry V's Chantry Chapel swamps the east end and in the aisles of Henry VII's Chapel are monuments to Elizabeth I and her rival, Mary Queen of Scots. This chapel, with its breathtaking fan vaulting, is a late addition to the Abbey: it was built 1503–12 for Henry VII as a Lady Chapel and houses the spectacular tomb designed for Henry and his queen, Elizabeth of York, by the Italian sculptor Pietro Torrigiano (the man who broke Michelangelo's nose); it is enclosed within a lavishly massive bronze screen.

The **Palace of Westminster** was a royal palace until the early 16th century, when Whitehall Palace became the preferred central London home of the royal family. The Palace of Westminster continued to house the law courts, the Houses of Parliament and various offices of government. The most important survival of the medieval palace is the gigantic Great Hall, built by William II 1097–9 and remodelled 1394–1401, when it was given its massive hammerbeam roof. It once housed the law courts and has many sombre associations: Edward II abdicated here; Charles I was condemned to death here; and here monarchs and other great men lie in state before their funerals. But it must have had its lighter moments: during a recent restoration a real-tennis ball made of horsehair was found trapped behind a beam in the ceiling, lost in a match four hundred years earlier.

Almost all the rest of the palace vanished forever in a great fire on 16 October 1834. The new building was designed by Charles Barry with the assistance of A.W.N. Pugin, who was responsible for the lavish decorative detail that adorns every possible surface. Between them they created one of the greatest masterpieces of 19th-century architecture – imposing and solemn, but lent a fairy-tale touch by its pinnacles and towers, most memorably recorded perhaps in Monet's famous paintings of the Thames. Little of the palace is accessible to the public, but patient queuing will gain admission to the public galleries of the House of Lords and House of Commons.

One of London's annual ceremonies is the state opening of Parliament in November, when the Queen rides to Westminster in a horse-drawn coach and, from the throne in the House of Lords, reads a speech outlining the legislation that the government intends to introduce in the coming year. She does not visit Westminster otherwise, a mark of the gulf between the Queen and her government that is at the heart of a constitutional monarchy. The court is situated elsewhere: domestically at Buckingham Palace and officially at the Tudor palace of St James's – officially, because although the Queen does not live there, it is 'to the Court of St James' that foreign ambassadors are accredited. **St James's Palace**, built by Henry VIII in the 1530s, is not open to the public, but it is possible to tour most of the exterior and to go to Sunday services in the Queen's Chapel, built 1626–7 to the designs of Inigo Jones. The gatehouse is Tudor, but most of the state rooms were added in the 17th century when Charles II made this his principal residence. It still provides a London home for some members of the royal family.

56 Below: *The Bank of England lies at the heart of the City of London, on the junction of most of its main streets. When the Bank was rebuilt (1921–37), the screen wall of the old building, by Soane, was retained. The Bank now rises seven storeys above the street and has three basement storeys. The statue of the Duke of Wellington is by Francis Chantrey (1844).*

57 Above: *St Paul's Cathedral from the south-east. The dome of Wren's masterpiece is a remarkable feat as much of engineering as of architecture. The drum carries an immense weight: the lantern and cross weigh 700 tons, while the dome itself weighs approximately 64,000 tons.*

Between the early 16th century, when the royal family moved out of Westminster Palace, and Charles II's settling in St James's a hundred and fifty years later, the principal royal residence was Whitehall Palace, which was burnt down in 1697 – all except the **Banqueting House** in Whitehall, designed by Inigo Jones and begun in 1619. This building announces the arrival of pure Renaissance classicism in British architecture. The exterior, revolutionary by the standards of the day, is probably barely noticed by the visitors who throng Whitehall to gaze at the mounted sentries outside Horse Guards opposite. Inside, the Banqueting House is a single white-and-gold double-cube room, with an unforgettable ceiling painted by Rubens. Here the Stuart kings entertained their guests and here, in 1649, on a scaffold erected in front of the hall, Charles I was beheaded.

That was probably the reason why Charles II preferred St James's. The royal homes built by Charles and his successors were modest by the standards of autocratic European monarchs. **Greenwich Palace** and **Hampton Court** (frontispiece), the first rebuilt and the second greatly extended in the late 17th century, were not modest, but Greenwich was from the beginning intended as a naval hospital, not a royal residence, and Hampton Court was barely used by kings in the 18th century. They preferred the quieter domesticity of **Kensington Palace** (**58**) and Kew. Matters changed somewhat with the arrival of the dissolute Prince Regent, later George IV, who in 1787 started the lavish redecoration of Carlton House in the Mall; by 1795 he had run up debts of £640,000 on it. In 1827–9 Carlton House was pulled down and **Carlton House Terrace** put up in its place. This vast stuccoed terrace was designed by the Regent's favourite architect, John Nash, and forms the stately opening of the **Mall**, the wide road which leads to the present-day principal residence of the monarch, **Buckingham Palace** (**59**).

In 1705 the Duke of Buckingham built a house for himself in what was then open country. George III purchased it in 1762, and in 1825 the Prince Regent instructed Nash to make plans for its rebuilding, which pushed ahead, resulting in debts as great as those incurred by the decoration of Carlton House. The expense was blamed partly on Nash, who was known for shady dealings in the building world. Little was actually proved against him, but after George IV's death in 1830 Nash was forced to retire and Buckingham Palace was completed by others. It has remained the monarch's London residence since Queen Victoria moved in in 1837; she is commemorated by the gigantic memorial that towers up at the end of the Mall. The palace's present façade is the result of rebuilding in 1913.

The palace faces greenery on both sides: to the rear are its extensive private gardens and to the front **Green Park** and **St James's Park**. London's parks are among her most precious amenities. Some, like St James's and **Kensington Gardens**, were once attached to royal residences; others, like **Hyde Park** and **Richmond Park**, were designed for hunting; some, like **Syon**, **Osterley** or **Chiswick**, are the pleasure grounds of aristocratic mansions now open to the public. Most are now devoted entirely to recreation; the grounds of Kew Palace, however, have been absorbed into the great botanical gardens of **Kew** (**67**), which since 1841 have been principally the national institution for botanical research and only secondarily one of the most beautiful landscaped parks in the country.

Whatever their origins, London's parks provide a welcome retreat from traffic and bustle; on a hot day they are irresistible. One of the most piquant

58 Below: *Kensington Palace, the home of Princess Margaret, seen from Kensington Gardens. The late-17th-century palace is open to the public. In the foreground is Princess Louise's statue of her mother, Queen Victoria, who was born in the palace in 1819. The statue was erected in honour of the Queen's Golden Jubliee.*

59 Right: *Buckingham Palace from St James's Park. On the right is the Queen Victoria Memorial; the Queen is shown in white marble on the base, below a gilded figure of Victory.*

sights in London is to be had from the low bridge that spans the lake in St James's Park. The view is encircled by the lofty monumental buildings of a great capital city, but they are only the backdrop to the trees, water, lawns and flower beds. The distant roar of traffic is blotted out by the calls of children and the noise of a very assorted flock of waterfowl, including several pelicans. The southern side of the park is lined by the backs of government offices in Whitehall and by the large parade ground of the **Horse Guards**, where every June the Trooping of the Colour takes place: a military display to mark the Queen's official birthday.

The conflagration that destroyed Whitehall Palace is one of many fires that have beset London through the centuries. The first, and one of the most horrible, was in AD61 when Queen Boudicca and her tribesmen ravaged the new city in the course of her unsuccessful rebellion against the Romans. A layer of ash, the result of her attack, has been discovered in the foundations of several buildings uncovered by archaeologists. The most famous blaze of all, the 'Fire of London', began in very different circumstances. On 2 September 1666 a fire broke out in a baker's shop on the corner of Pudding Lane in the City. Four days later almost two-thirds of London had been destroyed: 89 churches, 400 streets, 13,200 houses and numerous public buildings. The most spectacular loss was London's medieval cathedral, St Paul's, which erupted into flames so fierce that at night schoolboys in Westminster could read books by their light. Rebuilding was rapid, although hopes for a grand scheme of ordered avenues proved impossible. The medieval street pattern was mostly retained, but the new buildings were largely of brick, not wood: half-timbered Elizabethan London had vanished for ever.

The rebuilding of the City's churches and cathedral was directed by one man, Christopher Wren. He supplied plans for all 51 of the new churches built in the City (although he was not always responsible for them after the initial design stage), and he was in sole charge of the new **St Paul's** (**57**), which was paid for by a special tax on coal, built of Portland Stone and capped by one of the most serenely beautiful domes in the world. Work began here in 1675, and the last stone in the lofty lantern was laid by Wren's son Christopher in 1710, on or shortly after the architect's 78th birthday. The vast, cool interior is still much as it was in Wren's day; the magnificent choir stalls (carved by Grinling Gibbons) and Jean Tijou's gorgeous wrought-iron screens are unforgettable. Since the end of the 18th century many splendid monuments have been installed, but no visitor should miss one modest memorial in the crypt: two tablets that mark Wren's grave, one bearing his famous epitaph, *Lector, si monumentum requiris, circumspice* ('Reader, if you want to see his monument, look around you').

The churches that Wren designed for the rebuilt City had to be fitted onto sites that varied widely in size and shape, allowing their architect freedom to experiment with style and plan. Twenty-four of Wren's City churches survive and a tour of them makes a very satisfying experience. Four choice examples can be seen easily in a walk from the Monument to St Paul's. **The Monument** is a huge column built 1671–6 to commemorate the Fire of London. There is a platform at the top (reached by 311 spiral stairs) which gives good views over the London skyline. Close by, in Lower Thames Street, is **St Magnus Martyr** (1671–6), a noble church with the richest woodwork in the City. Behind the Mansion House (the home of the Lord Mayor) is **St**

60 *St Margaret Lothbury. Wren's church of 1686–90 replaces an early medieval building. The richly furnished interior is dominated by the superb chancel screen, made for the now demolished All Hallows the Great, to which it was presented by a German merchant, Theodore Jacobsen. The brass chandeliers are typical of 17th-century church interiors.*

Exodus Chap. XX.

Ceremonial London:
61 (above) *Inspection of the Yeoman Warders ('Beefeaters') outside the Queen's House in the Tower of London. They are wearing their royal livery, a red tunic trimmed with gold and a white ruff, worn only on special occasions. The Yeoman Gaoler at the end of the line holds the axe which used to be carried beside prisoners going to and from their trials.*
62 (below) *The Lord Mayor's Show. The procession sets out from the Mansion House, and travels down Poultry and Cheapside, past St Paul's, and then along Ludgate Hill and Fleet Street; it returns along the Embankment and Queen Victoria Street. The lavishly decorated Lord Mayor's coach, built in 1757, is accompanied by Pikemen and Musketeers of the Honourable Artillery Company, which always provides the Lord Mayor's bodyguard.*

OVERLEAF

63 Left: *The College of Arms was founded by Richard III to provide a home for the heralds, whose main work now concerns matters of genealogy and precedent. The present building was erected 1671–88; the royal coat of arms surmounts the porch.*

64 Right: *Goldsmiths' Hall, Foster Lane (1835), designed by Philip Hardwick, is probably the most impressive hall of any of the livery (guild) companies. Its rich monumentality reflects the wealth of the company, which can trace its history back to the 12th century.*

Stephen Walbrook (1672–9), which many regard as Wren's finest church: it has an ingenious Baroque steeple (added in 1717) and a centralised interior with a coffered dome. A short stroll along Poultry leads to what is perhaps the most celebrated City church of all, **St Mary-le-Bow**: its famous steeple contains the Bow bells (native Londoners, known as 'Cockneys', are traditionally defined as people born within sound of Bow bells). Finally, in Gresham Street is **St Anne and St Agnes** (1676–80), a charming, homely church that shows how much Wren was influenced by Dutch architecture.

This brief tour also leads past other important buildings in the City, notably the cluster around the **Bank of England** (**56**), where eight streets meet: Bank itself, **Mansion House** and the **Royal Exchange**. Close by is the **Stock Exchange**, and some spectacular modern buildings house other great financial institutions – look out for Richard Rogers' high-tech extravaganza for Lloyds (opened in 1986). Also at Bank is **St Mary Woolnoth** (1716–24), an extraordinarily powerful composition by Wren's most brilliant pupil, Nicholas Hawksmoor, who was responsible for a series of remarkable London churches, in Bloomsbury and the East End, at Stepney, Limehouse and Spitalfields.

Trips to **Spitalfields** or the further reaches of the East End will reveal how much London has depended on immigrant communities: the Georgian houses of Spitalfields, for instance, once housed silk weavers, the descendants of Huguenots who had fled persecution in France. In the City itself, important traces of these communities survive: Lombard Street's name is a reminder of the Italian origin of many merchants working in the medieval city, and at Bevis Marks is the **Spanish and Portuguese Synagogue**, built 1700–1 and superbly furnished and preserved.

Few people live in the City today, but some sense of what it must have felt like when many communities lived side by side, busily working together but maintaining their own identities, can be felt by a stroll through **Soho**, still London's most cosmopolitan area. Modern redevelopment has intruded in one or two places, but on the whole nowhere else gives such a strong sense of London's atmosphere before so much was rebuilt in the 19th and 20th centuries. The streets are narrow, interrupted only by two squares, the scale is domestic and the architecture is basically Georgian: walk through Meard Street, for instance – a scruffy backwater lined with unspoilt houses of 1732. In Soho are many of London's best restaurants – Chinese, Malay, Italian, Greek, French – as well as fashionable bars and shops, jazz clubs, the best grocers and fishmongers in central London and two excellent street markets: Berwick Street, cheap, noisy and Cockney, and Rupert Street, quieter, a little more exotic and expensive. Soho's raffish, even seedy atmosphere may not last much longer and, as property prices continue to rise, may lose its centuries-old function of housing the poor, the foreign, the newly arrived. It is an odd experience, when passing a sandwich bar or a shop blaring heavy metal music from a Georgian cul-de-sac, to note a blue plaque commemorating a brief stay by Shelley or Rimbaud.

Soho's atmosphere has proved remarkably resilient: that of **Covent Garden** (**66**), on the opposite side of the Charing Cross Road, has changed out of all recognition in a very short time. Its name probably evokes first the Opera House, the home of the Royal Opera and Ballet companies. This grand building, designed by E.M. Barry, is the third theatre on the site, replacing

COLLEGE OF ARMS

JUSTITIA
REGINA

one burned down in 1856. But from 1670 until 1973 Covent Garden also housed London's daily wholesale fruit, flower and vegetable market. The old market building designed by Charles Fowler Senior was built 1828–30; flowers were sold in the Floral Hall (1858–60), a glass and iron building next to the Opera House. When the market moved out, comprehensive redevelopment was threatened but largely averted. New buildings, none very distinguished, have gone up, but the old street pattern and most of the old buildings have been preserved. Covent Garden is now London's most newly fashionable area: the market building houses tiny shops selling clothes, books and food; the porters' cafés have been replaced by winebars and conversation in the pubs is more likely to concern video companies and designer clothes than the price of cabbages. This is the area in which to buy the latest in fashion and design and to sample London's most innovative restaurants.

The market building was put up in the centre of London's first square, 'the Piazza', laid out by Inigo Jones for the Earl (later Duke) of Bedford in the 1630s. Not a trace of this scheme remains today, with the exception of the Church of St Paul's, whose portico now houses Punch and Judy shows and other entertainers who cluster around Covent Garden. In fact, since the portico had to be at the east end, its big door is a sham: the entrance is at the other end, and is reached through a charming hidden garden. The piazza heralded the square, perhaps London's most characteristic urban feature. During the 18th century squares sprang up throughout the city, their design allowing often comparatively modest houses to be grouped together in one monumental composition. The garden that usually enlivens the middle of a

65 Below: *Cornwall Terrace (1821), one of the splendid stuccoed terraces designed by John Nash which are such a memorable feature of Regent's Park.*

66 Above: *The Punch and Judy public house on the lower level of Covent Garden, the home during three centuries of London's daily wholesale fruit, flower and vegetable market and now its most newly fashionable venue. The pub was opened in 1980, so named because it is near the site of the first English performance of a Punch and Judy show.*

square may be open only to residents of the surrounding houses; but in central London, where few private home-owners remain, it is often public. The most splendid of these domestic squares is **Bedford Square** in Bloomsbury, built *c.*1775, which uniquely has all four sides remaining.

At the beginning of the 19th century more systematic efforts were made to bring town planning to London. One of the most ambitious was John Nash's **Regent Street**, designed to connect Regent's Park with the Prince Regent's principal residence, Carlton House. Regent Street has been rebuilt and Carlton House has vanished, but the street plan remains, together with a principal focus, **All Souls**, Langham Place, whose circular porch was designed by Nash to harmonise the awkward junction between his two major streets, Portland Place and Regent Street. Nash was also responsible for the conception of **Trafalgar Square**, although none of its architecture is his. The name of this famous square commemorates Lord Nelson's triumph over the French fleet at Cape Trafalgar in 1805, where he was killed in the moment of victory. The admiral stands atop his column (167 feet 6½ inches high), which was erected in 1842. The four bronze lions round the base were modelled by the Victorian painter Edwin Landseer and cast in 1858.

Facing the column to the north is the long low classical façade of the **National Gallery**, founded in 1842. It contains the national collection of paintings, including many world-famous masterpieces, but only a handful of British pictures. British painting can be seen at the **Tate Gallery**, on Millbank, which is also a museum of 20th-century art. The creation of the National Gallery was one result of the great 19th-century drive to spread art and learning beyond the confines of the moneyed classes. Before then most museums had been private, and many of London's most distinguished small collections, such as the **Dulwich Picture Gallery** and **Sir John Soane's Museum**, began as private collections. One of the chief pleasures of a stay in London is the opportunity to visit one of these less-frequented museums, such as the **Wallace Collection** in Manchester Square, a glorious assembly of largely 18th-century French furniture and painting in an aristocratic Victorian mansion (it is also the home of Frans Hals' *Laughing Cavalier*).

The major forerunner of the Victorian public galleries and museums is the

67 *Kew Gardens' huge Temperate House was designed by Decimus Burton and took nearly forty years to build (1860–99). It is a long rectangular structure with north and south wings linked to a main building by octagonal vestibules. It was intended primarily as a winter garden and is designed so that the roof can be opened in hot weather.*

British Museum. Now housed in an imposing neoclassical building (1823–47) by Robert Smirke, it was originally set up in 1753 and was opened to the general public in the early 19th century. It contains one of the world's greatest collections of antiquities (the vast ethnographical collection is now at the **Museum of Mankind** in Burlington Gardens). Also in the building is the British Library, whose choicest treasures of books and manuscripts are on public display.

The major concentration of museums in London is in South Kensington. Here is the **Victoria and Albert Museum**, which houses the national collection of decorative arts and design. Next door are the **Science** and **Geological Museums** and the **Natural History Museum**, opened in 1881, a spectacular terracotta-clad extravaganza designed by Alfred Waterhouse. Their presence here is a result of the success of the Great Exhibition of 1851, the first major international display of technology and manufactures, held in Hyde Park at the instigation of Queen Victoria's husband, Prince Albert. He

68 Left: *The tea-clipper* Cutty Sark *(1869), now moored at Greenwich, was one of the last merchant sailing ships.*

69 Above: *The Albert Memorial, designed by Sir George Gilbert Scott, in honour of Queen Victoria's husband, who died in 1861. In Scott's words, the Prince is 'surrounded by works of sculpture illustrating those arts and sciences which he fostered'.*

is commemorated by the celebrated **Albert Memorial** (**69**) in Kensington Gardens, opposite the great circular **Albert Hall**, where the famous Promenade Concerts are held each summer.

A tour of any one of these museums will comfortably take at least a whole day, and is perhaps best followed by a visit to another great terracotta building – **Harrods**, London's most famous store, only a few minutes' walk away down the Brompton Road. Although the luxurious teas served here may seem rather alien to the high-minded culture of South Kensington, the combination of magnificent museums and smartly elegant shops attracts the crowds just as Albert's great exhibition did in 1851.

CONCERTS 1980

Oxford

The medieval chronicler Geoffrey of Monmouth included Oxford among the cities subject to King Arthur, but the first attested reference to the town is dated 912, when Edward the Elder of the Kingdom of Wessex took it as a stronghold against the Danes. Oxford probably originated as a settlement around St Frideswide's Priory, remains of which have been found under Christ Church. But the town owes its importance to its location at a major crossing-point of the Thames, most likely near the present Magdalen Bridge, and to the navigability of its two rivers – the Thames downstream to London, and the Cherwell to the Midlands. From earliest times Oxford was a market town, and today the width of **St Giles** and **Broad Street** reflects their use as medieval market sites.

The earliest building wholly visible and in use is the Saxon tower of **St Michael's Church**, built in the first half of the 11th century. By 1066 the town had 11 churches and about 1000 houses, making it the sixth largest in England. The Normans established their control over it by erecting the fortified castle: the mound and the tower of St George-in-the-Castle can still be seen.

70 *St Mary's Church: the South Porch (1637), designed by Nicholas Stone. Despite the fashionable baroque exterior, inside the porch there is a Gothic fan vault. Stone possibly copied the twisting columns from Raphael's tapestry cartoon 'The Healing of the Lame Man in the Temple' in the set purchased by Charles I and now in the Victoria and Albert Museum, London. The porch was paid for by Dr Owen, chaplain to Archbishop Laud, the University's Chancellor; the inclusion of a statue of the Virgin outraged Puritan opinion and formed one of the charges against Laud at his trial. During the Civil War it was damaged by the shots of a disapproving Parliamentarian soldier.*

Under the Normans religious foundations were established which began to attract scholars willing to teach as well as study. Their residence in Oxford is first documented before 1117, and as their numbers grew the University imperceptibly came into being. From the beginning there was endemic tension between 'town' and 'gown', between those who worked for a living and those who studied and prayed; and the poor discipline of the students was a constant problem. (In 1209 an anti-University riot caused some scholars to abandon Oxford for the refuge of the fens of East Anglia, thereby creating the University of Cambridge.) The building of a royal palace at Woodstock also drew scholars to the area, and the University benefited enormously from royal and ecclesiastical favour. In spite of the animosity of the town, then, learning flourished, and already in the 13th century Oxford had a European reputation for its teaching of mathematics and natural sciences.

Conflict between town and gown reached its height in the famous St Scholastica's Day riot of 1355, which began with a banal tavern brawl and ended with the death of 63 scholars. In the outcome the town paid a large fine to the University, which also gained the power to control the civic markets and assess rents. The Mayor and bailiffs were compelled to attend an annual Mass for the souls of the scholars slain in the riot – a penance not finally abolished until 1825.

The decline in the town's wealth and position during the 14th and 15th centuries was largely a result of the contraction of the wool trade and the devastation of the Black Death. The townspeople must have felt that a major cause was the tyrannical position of the University, which came to own most

of central Oxford; it also controlled much of its commerce, and by generating jobs made the town more and more dependent on it.

From this point onward therefore the history of Oxford is the history of the University. But during the Civil War the town unexpectedly became the Royalist capital, in addition to being England's oldest centre of learning: Charles I arrived in 1642 and held court here for the next three and a half years, until the city was captured by the Parliamentarians. The University loyally supported the King; but the town, like most merchant communities, favoured the Parliamentarian cause. Magdalen and New Colleges were turned into arsenals, provisions were stored in Brasenose and uniforms were made in the Astronomy School. Most of the colleges gave their gold and silver plate to be melted down and struck into coin at the emergency mint established in Oxford (though Corpus managed to preserve its famous collection).

It was only in the 19th century that the town recovered an economic life of its own, encouraged by the arrival of the railway in 1843. New residential areas were opened, further stimulated after 1877 when the University lifted its restrictions on dons, who now were able to marry and have families. In this century local industry developed in the most surprising way, when William Morris, originally a repairer of bicycles, turned to the manufacture of an automobile, the Morris Oxford. This was so successful that he established a factory at Cowley, east of the city, which by 1925 was making 41 per cent of all cars produced in the United Kingdom. His success attracted other industries to Oxford, and brought such wealth that by 1936 it was one of the

71 Above: *The Botanic Garden: the entrance archway (1632–3) by Nicholas Stone, bearing portraits of (left) Charles I, (right) Charles II and (top) the garden's creator, Henry Danvers, Earl Danby.*

72 Right: *The Schools Quadrangle: the tower of the five orders, so called because each tier has one of the five classical orders of columns. On the penultimate tier James I hands copies of his works to Fame and to the University; at the top is the royal coat of arms. In the foreground is a bronze statue of the 3rd Earl of Pembroke, Chancellor 1617–30.*

most prosperous towns in England. The Morris works at Cowley are still Oxford's largest employer. Morris, later Lord Nuffield, founded a graduate college (see below) and was in other ways a great benefactor of the University, particularly its medical department, but locally he is celebrated for restoring the fortunes of the city after it had lived for four hundred years in the shadow of one of the world's great universities.

The University is an accretion of colleges, which accumulated sporadically. From medieval times instruction was offered by clerics, who were supported by their own orders. The undergraduates lived in halls of residence, paying their own expenses and those of their instructor. **St Edmund Hall** was one such lodging. It had no individual founder, but was set up by a group of graduates who maintained the buildings as a boarding-house for undergraduates. It had no endowment, and was financed entirely by undergraduates' fees. But so many years of study were required to attain the degree in the higher faculties of law, theology or medicine that some means of support needed to be invented. This was the reason for the founding of the first colleges, which were endowed. The first organised college was **Merton** (**81**), founded in 1264 (its 14th-century Mob Quad is the oldest quadrangle in Oxford); **University College** was in existence by *c.*1280 and **Balliol** followed in 1282. Others – **Trinity**, **St John's** and **Worcester College** – have their origins in monastic educational establishments dissolved by Henry VIII.

Until the 16th century the colleges were mainly small and select communities of postgraduates – as **All Souls** (founded 1437) has remained to this day. But in 1379 **New College** (**79, 80**), the first Oxford college to accommodate undergraduates, was founded by William of Wykeham, Chancellor of England, Bishop of Winchester, and the richest prelate in England. His college far

73 Above: *Oxford's famous skyline (seen here from Carfax Tower) inspired Matthew Arnold's description in 'Thyrsis' of 'that sweet city with her dreaming spires' and Gerard Manley Hopkins' more accurate evocation of the 'Towery city' in 'Duns Scotus's Oxford'. Left to right: the tower of the Schools Quadrangle, New College bell-tower, the dome of the Radcliffe Camera, the towers of All Souls College (and the new Radcliffe Infirmary in the far distance), St Mary's spire and All Saints' Church.*

74 Right: *The Radcliffe Camera (1737–49), seen from St Mary's tower.*

75 Above: *Hertford College: the Bridge of Sighs (1913–14) over New College Lane links Hertford's two quads. Sir Thomas Jackson's design resembles the Venetian Bridge of Sighs (which prisoners crossed from the Doge's Palace to the gaol) much more closely than does its Gothic Cambridge counterpart* (**39**)*. New College bell-tower is visible behind the bridge.*

exceeded in size and wealth any previous foundation at Oxford or Cambridge. William intended New College to supply the Church with parish priests to make good the heavy losses caused by the Black Death. To ensure that the students had a thorough early education William made his college a dual foundation with a new grammar school at Winchester – now Winchester College (see page 120) – from which it took all its scholars (providing the model for King's College, Cambridge, which is linked to Eton).

In time other colleges began to accommodate undergraduates, some ostentatiously. **Christ Church** (**77**), founded by Cardinal Wolsey in 1525, has the largest quad, the biggest pre-Victorian hall, and its own art gallery; its chapel, which dates from 1194, is Oxford Cathedral. Christ Church's alumni have included 18 English Prime Ministers, as well as such eminent figures as the writer Sir Harold Acton, the poet W. H. Auden, and the composer Sir William Walton.

The religious commitment inspired by the Oxford Movement made a permanent mark on the establishment of **Keble College** (**76**) in 1870, the first new college in Oxford for over a century. It was named after the Revd John Keble, a religious poet and one of the founders of the Movement. A completely secular innovation was **Ruskin College** (1899), founded to make the privileges of an Oxford education available to working men and women. Like several foundations in the city it is informally affiliated with the University but not part of it; it is financed and governed by trade unions and other workers' organisations.

The most significant foundations in the 19th century were those for women.

Women had been associated with Oxford for centuries in the founding and endowment of men's colleges. But they were not admitted for education, and Cambridge first opened the door with the establishment of Girton College (see page 55). Subsequently two colleges were founded at Oxford specifically for women, **Lady Margaret Hall** and **Somerville**, in spite of strong opposition from the dons. Two others followed before the end of the century, **St Hugh's** (1886) and **St Hilda's** (1893). By 1894 all University examinations were open to women, although University degrees were not bestowed until 1920, and women's colleges did not achieve full collegiate status until 1959. Recently tradition has been entirely swept aside: the men's colleges have been opened to women, a much larger proportion of women has come to be admitted than before, and today only two single-sex colleges remain: St Hilda's and Somerville for women.

A particular feature of the 20th century has been the establishment of graduate colleges, among them **Nuffield College**, founded as long ago as 1937 as a centre of research 'especially by cooperation between academic and non-academic people', and **Green College**, devoted to the postgraduate study of medicine.

It is not known when the colleges were first thought to constitute a coherent unit, but the first reference to a University Chancellor occurs in 1214, indicating some sort of organised University by then. The earliest focus of University activities was the **Church of St Mary the Virgin** (**70**); here the archives were stored, ceremonies took place and Congregation (the governing body) convened.

76 Below: *Keble College, designed by William Butterfield. Liddon Quad, dominated by the college's huge chapel (1868–82), exemplifies the architect's passion for polychromatic brickwork. Ruskin gave up his daily walks in the Parks to avoid having to look at it.*

77 Left: *Christ Church: Tom Tower. The upper part, designed by Wren, was added to the gate built in the time of the founder, Cardinal Wolsey. Wolsey's statue was placed over the gate in 1872. In the foreground are (left) St Aldate's Church and (right) Pembroke College.*

78 Right: *Summer in Magdalen Deer Park: fallow deer grazing and resting in the shade. Magdalen, founded in 1458 outside the city walls, has extensive and beautiful grounds.*

OVERLEAF

Left: *New College:*
79 (above) *The garden of the 14th-century cloister.*
80 (below) *Inside the cloister.*

81 Right: *Merton College: the gateway (1418) onto Merton Street.*

The University received gifts of books from the beginning of the 13th century. In the 15th century the new interest in classical learning was stimulated and encouraged by such gifts as the manuscripts from Henry V's brother Duke Humphrey, and in 1478 the first Oxford book was printed. Duke Humphrey's collection was dispersed in the 16th century, but Thomas Bodley, diplomat and Fellow of Merton, assembled two thousand books to form the basis of a new library, opened in 1602. The **Bodleian Library** is today one of the greatest in the world, and its holdings of manuscripts and early printed books are surpassed in this country only by those of the British Library. On the day of Bodley's funeral in 1613 building began on the **Schools Quadrangle** (**72**). Lectures and examinations were held here until the 19th century, when the sharp rise in undergraduate numbers led to the building of the Examinations Schools, between Merton Street and the High Street.

Oxford's reception of Renaissance classical scholarship is reflected in the statutes of **Corpus Christi College**, founded in 1512, with a provision for professors of Latin and Greek who would deliver lectures to the whole University. In fact the emphasis at Corpus was not so much on classical scholarship as on creating a college that could produce educated clergymen. As a centre of theological learning the University became embroiled in the religious disputes of the 15th and 16th centuries, of which the most dreadful result was the death of Archbishop Cranmer and Bishops Ridley and Latimer, burnt at the stake in St Giles, where the **Martyrs' Memorial** now stands.

During Elizabeth I's reign it became fashionable for the gentry and

aristocracy to send their sons to Oxford as the preliminary step to a career in politics and the civil service. Learning flourished: although theology was still pre-eminent, geography, mathematics, archaeology and astronomy were all studied with enthusiasm. Yet at the same time the level of scholarship and instruction was very uneven. Edward Gibbon, author of *Decline and Fall of the Roman Empire*, recalled that the 14 months that he spent at Magdalen (1752–3) were 'the most idle and unprofitable of my whole life... the Fellows of my time were decent, easy men... their days were filled by... the chapel and the hall, the coffee-house and the common-room, till they retired, weary and well satisfied, to a long slumber. From the toil of reading or thinking or writing they had absolved their conscience.'

By the 17th century many churchmen felt that St Mary's should not house noisy secular University ceremonies, and the Chancellor, Archbishop Sheldon, financed the building of a theatre for such functions. The **Sheldonian Theatre** (1663–9), designed by the young Christopher Wren, was the first classical building in Oxford, shaped like a Roman theatre. Ever since its opening, major University ceremonies and concerts have been held here – in 1733 Handel played the organ for the first performance of his *Athalia*.

The University's lax attitude to religious observance stimulated John and Charles Wesley to initiate what became one of the world's great Christian movements, Methodism – though while they were still at Oxford their piety took the form of High-Church zeal, to the distaste of the orthodox dons. Their enthusiasm was at least preferable to religious denial: University College's most famous undergraduate, the poet Shelley, was expelled in 1811 for publishing a pamphlet entitled *The Necessity of Atheism*.

The University at last began to reform itself in the 19th century. The modern examination system was instituted in 1801, but at first only a minority of undergraduates took the exams. In 1850 a Royal Commission

82, **83** *Two contrasting faces of Oxford in summer:* (below) *Punts on the Cherwell and* (right) *The annual ceremony of the Encaenia: Lord Stockton (Harold Macmillan), Chancellor of the University 1960–86, processing to the Sheldonian Theatre to confer honorary degrees. In front are the Bedels, carrying their 16th-century maces. The procession is about to enter the Schools Quadrangle through the main gateway, which is opened only on ceremonial occasions.*

criticised Oxford for its failure to encourage either learning or research. This was in part a result of the energy spent on theological controversy, especially in connection with the Oxford Movement. The leaders of the movement, Keble, Pusey, Newman and Froude, wished to rid Oxford of its worldliness and persuade the colleges to inculcate their students with spiritual and moral awareness. Their theology appeared to be tinged with Catholicism, which made them unpopular, and when in 1845 Newman was received into the Roman Catholic Church the Movement lapsed. The secularisation of Oxford education was completed by the abolition (1871) of the religious test which students formerly had to take before receiving their degrees.

As theological dispute ceased to dominate University affairs interest turned to newer subjects. As early as 1677 the University had acquired from Elias Ashmole the collection assembled by John Tradescant of geological and zoological specimens from around the world, together with coins, books and engravings. The antiquities were ultimately deposited in the **Ashmolean Museum** (1845), which today houses the Arundel Marbles (the celebrated group of classical sculptures assembled by the Earl of Arundel in the early 17th century), a major collection of coins, and an outstanding collection of old-master paintings and drawings. The magnificant cast-iron **University Museum** was begun in 1855 to house examples of 'all the materials explanatory of the organic being placed upon the globe'; the **Pitt Rivers Museum** of ethnography was added in 1885–6.

In the last half of the 19th century undergraduate and research student numbers rose dramatically. Having for long been chiefly devoted to preparing men for the Church, Oxford turned into a forcing-house for the professions – medicine, law, politics, teaching and the civil service – and educated the men who ran the Empire. Numerous student societies were founded – literary, musical, theatrical, drinking and political – many quite ephemeral. The most famous is the Oxford Union (founded 1825), traditionally a nursery for aspiring politicians; its past presidents include Gladstone, Asquith and Edward Heath. Organised games were encouraged, and the Oxford of popular mythology, a place of punts and champagne, boaters and *Charley's Aunt*, took root. Evelyn Waugh, an undergraduate at **Hertford College** during the 1920s, gives an acid description of Oxford life of that period in the opening chapter of his first novel, *Decline and Fall*, and a much less acid one in the first part of *Brideshead Revisited*.

Today the spirit of the place is charged with an academic earnestness that Waugh's characters would hardly recognise. But old customs survive in the old surroundings. Perhaps the best known, because the public attends, is the traditional choral singing from the top of Magdalen College tower, Oxford's most famous landmark, at 6 a.m. every May Day. This was originally a prolonged and jolly secular concert; a religious element was introduced in the late 18th century, when the choir adopted the present custom of singing part of the college's Latin grace. Large crowds gather to listen from punts on the river, and the ceremony is followed by bell-ringing and morris dancing, and champagne breakfasts for those who have been up all night.

The titular head of the University is the Chancellor, usually an eminent statesman or member of the royal family; in 1987 Roy Jenkins, formerly President of the European Commission, succeeded Harold Macmillan. Actual authority is exercised by the Vice-Chancellor, who is elected every four years and is usually the head of one of the colleges. The relationship between the

84 Below: *Worcester College: the 15th-century south range, which was originally part of the monastic Gloucester College, dissolved in 1541. After a chequered history, the building became part of the new Worcester College at its foundation in 1714.*

85 Above: *The wide expanse of Christ Church meadow affords magnificent views of the colleges that border it. Left to right: Christ Church: the pinnacles on the hall, Bodley's bell-tower, Tom Tower* (**77**) *and the spire and chancel of Oxford Cathedral, which is also Christ Church's chapel (the rose window was installed in 1853); Corpus Christi College: the Fellows' Building (1706–16); and Merton College: the Grove Building.*

University and the colleges is vague and informal. Traditionally the organisation of teaching and the curriculum is a matter for the colleges and the faculties. The colleges are self-governed, by the Master and Fellows, in no way administered by the University. Each college has its own statutes, which can be altered only with the consent of the Queen in Council. Although the University is the degree-giving body the colleges' obligations to it do not go much beyond setting aside a portion of their Fellowships for professors and paying an annual tax whereby the richer colleges, such as Magdalen and Christ Church, subsidise the poorer. The colleges live off their endowments; the University receives its income directly from the government.

Undergraduates are selected by the college to which they apply, not by the University. The usual undergraduate course lasts three years, except for Classics – known as Greats – which takes four. Most undergraduates live in college for at least one and usually two years; for the rest of the time they live out in college-owned hostels or lodgings. The colleges are responsible for individual tuition, and every college provides teaching in almost every subject in small 'tutorials'. Lectures in the faculties, and laboratory work, are arranged by the University, as are the degree examinations or 'Schools'. Those who have done well in their Schools may stay on in Oxford as research students. All alumni are eligible for the award of the MA (Master of Arts) degree: all MAs resident in Oxford, whether associated with the University or not, are entitled to vote in meetings of Congregation, a remarkable example of academic democracy, and of the bonds which tie the students to the University (and in affection to their colleges) for life.

86 *Shakespeare's monument (on the north wall of the chancel of Holy Trinity Church), erected to Stratford-upon-Avon's most famous citizen soon after his death in 1616, with his coat of arms above. The first two lines of his epitaph can be translated 'In judgement a Nestor, in wit a Socrates, in art a Virgil / The earth covers him, the people mourn him. Olympus has him'. 'SIEH' in the penultimate line is the stonecutter's mistake for 'SITH'.*

Stratford-upon-Avon

Stratford's fame has spread worldwide as the town where William Shakespeare was born. The plan of the centre has changed little since his time, low timbered Tudor and red-brick Georgian buildings still lining the streets. On a bright morning the busy shops are reminders that for five hundred years Stratford has been a market town, the oldest in Warwickshire.

Its history begins with the Roman occupation, but it was during the Middle Ages that Stratford flowered. The Gild of the Holy Cross, which consisted of prominent townsfolk, boasted its own **Gild Chapel** (**87**), where a chaplain prayed for the members' souls while they looked to the town's earthly needs, supporting a school, almshouses and charities. The chapel's small early-15th-century chancel is overshadowed by the impressive late-15th-century nave. The spareness of the simple white interior contrasts markedly with the wealth of the founders. Wall-paintings showing the legend of the Holy Cross, from which the Gild took its name, were whitewashed over in 1563. Parts survive, the clearest being the Last Judgement, above the chancel arch.

Next to the chapel looms the L-shaped two-storeyed **Grammar School** (**88**), built in 1417 as the Guildhall in the form of two half-timbered halls. The school was considered to be one of the best in the county. Sons of local dignitaries were allowed free education and since Shakespeare's father was bailiff (mayor), young William probably studied here. You can see his desk at his birthplace.

In the 15th century typical Warwickshire houses were constructed of red brick with timber frames. A well-preserved example is **Mason's Court** (**91**) in Rother Street. The High Street's magnificent timbered **Harvard House** has survived since 1595, when it was partly rebuilt after a fire. The initials on the exterior are the owners', Thomas and Anne Rogers, whose grandson John Harvard gave his name to the American university. Harvard House is also known as The Garrick Inn after the famous 18th-century Shakespearean actor, who presented the statue of the playwright gracing the honey-coloured Town Hall. In the same street a less congenial place to stay was **The Cage** or gaol, now the Tourist Information Centre.

Shakespeare's father married Mary Arden and by 1552 they had moved to what is now known as the **Birthplace** (**89**), living in the left-hand portion of the house and establishing a glove-making business next door. Set in a garden now planted with flowers mentioned in Shakespeare's plays, this substantial old building is constructed of wood from the nearby Forest of Arden and stone from the local Wilmcote quarry. The dark, low rooms with their massive hearths seem frozen in time despite the buses which pass just outside the little leaded windows. Upstairs troops of visitors have venerated the spot where Shakespeare was born (**96**). Tennyson and Scott are among the many who have scratched their names in homage on the windowpanes.

OVERLEAF

87 Above left: *The 15th-century nave and tower of the Gild Chapel. The clipped hedges in the foreground belong to the great garden of New Place, which in Shakespeare's time formed the orchard and kitchen garden of his last home. Left of the chapel is the rear of the Grammar School (1417), which Shakespeare probably attended.*

88 Below left: *The school's Church Street frontage.*

89 Above right: *Shakespeare's birthplace from its garden, which is planted with flowers mentioned in his plays. On the gravel path is the foundation stone of Stratford's medieval market cross.*

90 Below right: *Looking from the Knot Garden (a modern reconstruction of a formal Elizabethan garden) behind the site of New Place towards the chimneys and gables of Nash's House, home of Shakespeare's granddaughter and her husband.*

Above: *Examples of Stratford's domestic architecture:*
91 (left) *Mason's Court, Rother Street, typical of 15th-century Warwickshire in its combination of red brick and timber framing.*
93 (right) *Hall's Croft in Old Town (late 16th century), probably the home of Shakespeare's daughter Susanna and her husband Dr John Hall.*

92 Left: *The graveyard of Holy Trinity Church in Old Town, the site of the earliest settlement at Stratford.*

A short distance away is the site of **New Place**. Bought by William Shakespeare as a retirement home, New Place was the second largest residence in town and the first to be made of brick. It had been erected during the reign of Henry VIII for Stratford's great benefactor, Sir Hugh Clopton, who paid for old Clopton Bridge to be rebuilt in stone. The mulberry in the garden is a cutting from the bard's own tree. Sadly the original, and the property itself, both suffered at the hands of an 18th-century owner, the Revd Francis Gastrell, who, irritated by droves of relentless sightseers, chopped down the tree and sold the wood for souvenirs. After a row about his rates he demolished the house too. The public outcry forced him to leave town. The foundations of New Place are all that remain of Shakespeare's last house. A pleached crab-apple walk leads to a sunken knot garden.

Nash's House, alongside the site of New Place, still stands. This lovely half-timbered residence was home to Shakespeare's granddaughter Elizabeth and her husband Thomas Nash. The upper floor contains a small museum; the rooms below are furnished in period style. Not far from here Shakespeare's eldest daughter Susanna and her husband Dr John Hall lived in the comfortably furnished **Hall's Croft** (**93**). In the charming walled back garden hollyhocks, lupins and cornflowers have superseded the doctor's medicinal herbs.

Walking for a mile across recreation fields brings you to the village of Shottery and **Anne Hathaway's Cottage** (**99**), a 12-roomed house, once the property of the wealthy farmers into whose family Shakespeare married. You can admire the parlour (**100**), see Anne's canopied bed – designed to protect

94 Above: *The Royal Shakespeare Theatre (opened 1932), overlooking the River Avon.*

95 Left: *a scene from a production by the Royal Shakespeare Company of Shakespeare's comedy* Love's Labour's Lost.

96 Right: *Shakespeare's birthplace: the room where Shakespeare is believed to have been born. Its Elizabethan furnishings were installed by the Birthplace Trust, which acquired the house in 1847.*

OVERLEAF

97 Above left: *Charlecote Park (1558), the earliest Elizabethan mansion in Warwickshire, was extensively rebuilt in the 19th century, but the fine porch retains its original masonry.*

98 Below left: *Mary Arden's House, Wilmcote, thought to have been the childhood home of Shakespeare's mother.*

99 Above right: *Anne Hathaway's Cottage at Shottery, childhood home of Shakespeare's wife.*

100 Below right: *The 'hall' or parlour of Anne Hathaway's Cottage, with its original open chimney.*

the sleeper from creatures tumbling out of the thatch – and then retreat to the secluded orchard and look out onto Warwickshire farmland. Shakespeare's mother came from Wilmcote, 3 miles outside Stratford; her 16th-century family home, now **Mary Arden's House** (**98**), is a museum of local agricultural life.

Back in the area of Old Town, the site of the earliest settlement at Stratford, there are memorials to Shakespeare's family in the splendid medieval **Church of the Holy Trinity**. The oldest parts of the church are the 13th-century transepts and upper sections of the tower. Lime trees flank the church path: 12 on one side for the tribes of Israel and 11 on the other for the faithful apostles. Inside, the chancel choir stalls are adorned with 26 fine misericords. These 15th-century carvings show camels, mermaids and wife-beaters. Shakespeare was probably baptised at the now broken font and his tombstone lies before the high altar. It bears the inscription: 'Good frend for Iesus sake forbeare / To digg the dust encloased heare / Blest be ye man yt spares thes stones / And curst be he yt moves my bones'. Shakespeare's wife, Susanna and John Hall and Thomas Nash are also buried here.

Leaving the riverside graveyard you can stroll townwards along the banks of the River Avon through the gardens of the Royal Shakespeare Theatre (**94**), built in 1932. The first Shakespeare theatre stood at the back of the New Place gardens from 1827 to 1872, but in 1874 two acres on the Avon's banks were allocated for a memorial theatre. This burnt down in 1926 but sixty years later the new Swan Theatre rose phoenix-like from the ruins: the Elizabethan-style auditorium was built within the Victorian shell and is dedicated primarily to performances of less familiar 16th- and 17th-century dramas.

Winchester

Winchester, once the capital of England, is now a quiet cathedral city with law courts, a barracks, an art school, a college of higher education and an ancient independent school. Around the old city of canons, colleges and colonels lies a sprawl of new housing and light industry; but the ancient core combines much 18th-century charm with reminders of the great periods of early English history.

Where the River Itchen can easily be crossed as it runs from the water meadows to the north through two highish chalk hills (St Giles' to the east and St Paul's to the west), a Celtic settlement existed before Romans or Anglo-Saxons came on the scene. The iron-age hill-fort and earthworks of St Catherine's Hill lie to the south-east of the city. Started in the 3rd century BC and abandoned two or three centuries later, they are the main relics of the Celtic Belgae.

The Romans appear to have reached Winchester soon after the Emperor Claudius' invasion of Britain in AD43. They built a walled city with four gates at north, east, south and west, and roads running from them to the Roman towns at Salisbury, Silchester and Southampton. The present High Street marks the *decumanus* of the Roman city, and a medieval gate still stands at the west end of it. Fragments of the city wall remain, and Roman house floors have been excavated in the city centre. The Roman name of the town was Venta Belgarum, which perhaps means the market place of the Belgae.

The departure of the Romans in the 5th century was followed by the resistance of the Romano-Celtic Britons to those invaders from the Continent called Angles, Saxons and Jutes. Legend makes King Arthur and his knights the heroes of this struggle. Romantics often see Winchester as King Arthur's Camelot. Scholars are sceptical, but Henry III's **Great Hall** at the top of the High Street still houses the medieval 'Round Table of King Arthur', which testifies to the antiquity of the legend, if not to its truth.

The greatness of Winchester as a capital city and as a centre of learning and religious foundations begins with the Saxons – the 'New English', as opposed to the 'Ancient Britons'. The Saxon King Cynegils, converted to Christianity by the missionary St Birinus in 635, began the process which turned Winchester into the holy city and capital of the West Saxon kings. Two great minster churches (Oldminster and Newminster), predecessors of the Norman cathedral, were built between *c.*660 and 904, together with a nunnery. The see of the bishopric of Wessex was moved here from Dorchester-on-Thames, so Winchester became the seat of Saxon bishops as well as of Saxon kings, and a great centre of Saxon Christian civilisation. The bones of five Saxon kings and two Saxon bishops rest to this day in reliquary chests in the Cathedral. The greatest of the bishops, St Swithun, died in 861 and was buried in Oldminster, of which the outline can be seen in the grass just north of the present

101 *'King Arthur's Round Table', 18 feet across and weighing more than a ton, now hangs on the west wall of the Great Hall. Certainly it was originally a table, with 12 legs supporting a rim and one in the middle. Constructed in the mid-13th century, it was painted for the first time in c.1520, and subsequently repainted, with a Tudor rose in the centre, the names of 24 knights of King Arthur round the edge and the figure of King Arthur at the top.*

Cathedral; his shrine was transferred here in 1093 and revered as a place of pilgrimage until it was destroyed at the Reformation. The greatest of the Saxon kings, Alfred, died in 899 and was buried in Newminster, which he had planned, close to Oldminster. Newminster was pulled down and transferred to Hyde Abbey, north of the city, in the 12th century; so Alfred's resting-place, like Swithun's, is lost. A thousand years after his death the great statue of King Alfred by Hamo Thornycroft was erected in the Broadway at the bottom of the High Street. St Ethelwold, Bishop of Winchester 936–86, in

collaboration with St Dunstan of Canterbury, reorganised the monastery as a Benedictine priory in 964.

When the Normans accepted the surrender of Winchester in November 1066, they were not total strangers to the city, nor was Winchester unused to strangers from the Continent. Edward the Confessor, the last Saxon king, was crowned in Winchester, but his mother was Emma of Normandy and her second husband was Canute the Dane. Emma's and Canute's bones lie among those of the Saxon kings in the Cathedral. Queen Edith, widow of Edward the Confessor and sister of Harold, lived on peaceably in Winchester once it had become the seat of a Norman king and a Norman bishop.

Of the palace, Royal Mint and Treasury of William I nothing remains today. The **Cathedral** (**102, 103**) was begun in 1079 by Bishop Wakelin and dedicated in 1093, replacing the adjacent Saxon Oldminster, which was pulled down as soon as the continuation of the Benedictine office could be transferred to the new building. The Norman parts of the Cathedral can still be seen in the tower, transepts and crypt. The tower indeed had to be rebuilt, for the wicked William Rufus was buried under it in 1100, and seven years later it collapsed in protest.

When Henry I died in 1135, leaving no living son, Winchester was at the eye of the succession storm. Henry de Blois, Bishop of Winchester and grandson of the Conqueror, backed the claim to the throne of his brother Stephen against their cousin Matilda. The Bishop's castle at Wolvesey became a fortified stronghold, the royal palace was burnt, chaos reigned and 'men said openly that Christ slept, and His saints'.

102 Above: *Winchester Cathedral from the roof of Winchester College Chapel, with the College's Middle Gate and Outer Gate in the foreground.*

103 Right: *The west front of Winchester Cathedral,* c.*1360–1400.*

Henry II of Anjou (1154–89), Matilda's son, brought back peace and order. Winchester and its wool trade flourished, enjoying the privileges of 18 royal charters bestowed between 1155 and 1561. The Cathedral, proprietor of manors stretching widely over southern England, had a full range of monastic buildings covering most of the present **Cathedral Close**. In the scriptorium the fine work of the Winchester school (its Benedictine traditions going back to the time of Alfred) reached a peak in the production of the Winchester Bible during the bishopric of Henry de Blois (1129–73). The splendour of the illuminated initials of this great manuscript can be admired in the Cathedral Library in the south transept.

In the 14th century a new disaster struck. The Black Death reached Winchester in 1348, and returned in 1361, 1369 and 1379. According to reports, threequarters of the population died in the first year of the plague. It was the start of a steady decline in the fortunes of the city. Nevertheless, out of the evil some good was to come.

William of Wykeham had become both Bishop of Winchester and Chancellor of England in 1367, and he set himself to replenish the diminished ranks of the clerkly, literate administrative class. From his own resources he founded New College in Oxford; then in 1382 he received from Richard II a royal charter to found **Winchester College** (**106–8**), which has some claim to be the oldest school in England in continuous operation in its original buildings.

Wykeham's predecessor, Bishop Edington, had begun the transformation of the Cathedral nave from rough Norman work to the new Perpendicular style. Leaving Edington's two westernmost bays, Wykeham converted the rest of the nave to its present soaring elegance. Those who regret the loss of a

104 Below: *The superb woodwork of Winchester Cathedral's choir stalls (1308), the oldest complete stalls in Britain, with all but two of their original misericords. In the foreground is the unmarked tomb of the despotic William Rufus (1056–1100), who succeeded his father, William the Conqueror, in 1087.*

105 Right: *This view down the south aisle, looking east, gives an idea of the amazing extent of Winchester Cathedral, the longest medieval cathedral in Europe (the nave measures 556 feet).*

Winchester College:
106 (above left) *A statue of the founder, William of Wykeham, in the niche above the doorway of School.*
107 (above right) *The 17th-century 'throne' in School, from which the Headmaster used to teach his class.*
108 (right) *Scholars of Winchester College, in their traditional black gowns, entering the hall in the south range of late-14th-century Chamber Court.*

Norman nave may perhaps be comforted by considering that what was lost was not the best Norman workmanship.

The great building – the longest medieval cathedral church in Europe – continued as a Benedictine monastic house up to the Reformation, and continued, too, its royal connections. Here Henry III was baptised in 1207 and Prince Arthur, elder brother of Henry VIII, in 1486; here King John was received back into Mother Church in 1213, and Henry IV married in 1403. Here also, at immense expense, Mary Tudor was married to Philip II of Spain on 25 July 1554.

The Reformation caused havoc in Winchester. It brought destruction to St Swithun's shrine in the Cathedral, and to the great west window (now jigsawed together); the statues in the reredos were broken, and the monastic buildings to the south (cloisters, dorter, refectory, etc.) disappeared. The Benedictine Priory was suppressed but the church survived as Winchester Cathedral. The Prior's lodging beame the Deanery but of the Chapter House only the Norman arcade remains.

The Civil War was the last of the disasters to befall Winchester. The Royalist city fell to Oliver Cromwell's guns, and Charles I came in chains to the old prison over the Westgate; but the citizens received the prisoner with all proper ceremony due to royalty. When Charles II was restored to his

throne, he started a palace at Winchester, designed by Christopher Wren, to show his respect for the ancient capital. This was on the site of the present Barracks (**109**), but fire destroyed the beginnings and it was never finished.

A visit to present-day Winchester should start at the top of the **High Street**, at the remains of the Norman royal castle. Henry III's Great Hall (1222–36) still stands, and above the remains of the royal dais hangs 'King Arthur's Round Table' (**101**), thought to have been built in the 13th or 14th century but repainted by order of Henry VIII, who proudly showed it to the Hapsburg Charles V as proof of the antiquity of the English throne. As you continue down the High Street you pass the medieval **Westgate**, where Charles I was imprisoned, and the 18th-century Guildhall (now Lloyds Bank), with a pleasant bracketed clock and statue of Queen Anne. As you approach the medieval **Butter Cross**, look at the distant statue of the Saxon **King Alfred** at the bottom of the High Street before turning through a narrow passage to your right. This will take you past the site of the palace of the Norman kings and lead you through a charming part of 18th-century Winchester to the Cathedral.

After your visit of the great building, walk through the **Cathedral Close** to the south, and in your mind's eye place around the grass the complex of Norman monastic buildings. Much of the old Priory remains in the present Deanery, whose grey arches look out onto the 17th-century brick of the Judges' Lodgings. To your left lies the **Pilgrims School**, its name remembering the medieval pilgrims to the shrine of St Swithun, who perhaps lodged in the ancient hall beside the present school. A tithe barn, where once the dues and produce owed to the Benedictine Priory were stored, leads you to the southern gate of the Close. As you pass through this, you are between the Cathedral Walk on your right and, on your left, 14th-century **Kingsgate**, which stands in the line of the old city wall.

Move now into **College Street**, and pass No. 8, the house where Jane Austen died in July 1817. She had come to Winchester two months earlier 'to

109 Above: *The Peninsula Barracks on Romsey Road (c.1900), the home of the Green Jackets Regiment until 1985.*

110 Right: *Beaufort Tower (c.1445), the gateway to St Cross, rising massively behind the 15th-century north range of the main quadrangle. To the left is the Elizabethan east range.*

111 *The brothers' quarters of St Cross, in the west range of the main quadrangle. Each entry leads to four three-room dwellings, two above and two below, which share a single high octagonal chimney-stack. The brothers of the original Order of Poverty still wear the centuries-old uniform of black cap and gown. The brothers of Cardinal Beaufort's Order of Noble Poverty (1446) wear claret-coloured caps and gowns.*

seek the medical advice of Mr Lydford', and it was here that she put the finishing touches to *Persuasion*. Soon you come to Outer Gate of **Winchester College**. William of Wykeham dedicated the school to the Blessed Virgin, whose 14th-century statue stands in a niche over the entrance. Call in and see Chamber Court (**108**), which has housed 70 scholars continuously since 1394. The period of construction of these ancient buildings coincides almost exactly with the years in which Chaucer was composing the *Canterbury Tales*.

At the end of College Street stands **Wolvesey**, a home for the bishops of Winchester designed by Sir Thomas Fitch (d. 1689), but little used by them until 1928, when they left their grander seat at Farnham. In the grounds of Wolvesey stand the remains of the castle built by Henry of Blois in the 12th century.

Now, if time and energy allow, walk southwards for ¾ mile through the water meadows past branches of the River Itchen, where mists rise over the low chalk streams. Here John Keats walked in the season of mists and mellow fruitfulness to compose his ode *To Autumn*. He would have seen, as you do, the Celtic hill fort of St Catherine's Hill rising roundly to his left, and ahead of him the squat Norman tower of St Cross.

A river path leads to the Hospital of **St Cross** (**110**, **111**), perhaps the loveliest of all Winchester's historic buildings. Here Henry de Blois founded in the 12th century a hospice for poor pensioners, who live college-wise round an ancient quadrangle dominated by a Norman chapel. Most of what you now see belongs to the re-foundation by Cardinal Beaufort in 1445. This great and good Bishop of Winchester is better remembered here in the peace of St Cross than in the market place of Rouen, where his emissaries consigned Joan of Arc to the flames.

St Cross is the setting for Anthony Trollope's early novel *The Warden*, published in 1855. Trollope was educated at Winchester College, and the troubles of Victorian St Cross were the starting-point of his series of Barchester novels on the convolutions of cathedral close politics.

Having walked to St Cross, you are entitled to claim the Wayfarer's Dole at the gateway to the Hospital. You will be given bread and a small measure of ale, and so properly end your visit with the taste of the Middle Ages on your lips.

York

The strategic benefits of a site at the centre of northern England where the Rivers Ouse and Foss flow together attracted Roman, Saxon and Viking invaders to settle. The seat of an archbishopric since 735, York has served as unofficial and sometimes official capital of the north.

Building began on the city's great **walls** (**112**) in the mid-13th century. As at all walled towns – few still exist – access was through patrolled gateways called 'bars'. (It is the streets which are 'gates', from the Norse word *gata*.) Four major gateways survive at York. **Monk Bar** lies to the east, commanding a fine view of the Minster. Under siege this 14th-century gatehouse functioned as a self-contained fortress.

A decree ruled that two tall men be stationed at the bars to question suspicious wayfarers. The guards at **Bootham Bar** must have been constantly on the alert, for the gate faces north, the direction from which attack was most likely. And for travellers the way was hazardous too, through the medieval Forest of Galtres, menaced by wild beasts. **Walmgate Bar** (**120**), to the west, preserves its original barbican, portcullis and gates, while to the south **Micklegate Bar** is capped by (replacement) token figures of knights to ward off danger. This is the traditional point of entry to the city for the sovereigns of England: the heads of monarchs have passed beneath this gate, and those of traitors have been stuck on poles above it.

112 *York's famous city walls in springtime, the mound covered with a mass of yellow daffodils. The walls were rebuilt in stone bewteen 1250 and 1315, as the previous wooden defences began to prove an inadequate guard against increasingly sophisticated warfare techniques. Much of the money needed for their construction was raised by a tax (known as Murage) levied on all goods entering the city. Despite the strenuous efforts of the City Corporation in the 19th century to have them demolished, most of the walls survive today, and have been well restored; they extend for over two miles, and a walk along the footpaths on top is one of the best ways to see the city.*

Walking along the walls from here you overlook the curved and cobbled **Micklegate**, favoured address of wealthy Georgian families. Pass the Victorian railway station (**117**) with its 800-foot curved roof supported by Corinthian pillars, and spy the twin towers of the Minster before the wall snakes down towards Lendal Bridge.

The Romans first fortified York to control local Celtic tribes. Their fortress covered about 50 acres where the Minster precincts now stand. In the **Museum Gardens** are sections of stone wall, including the ten-sided **Multangular Tower**, whose red-tiled base is 4th century. The part with arrow-slits is late 13th century and adjoins a 150-foot stretch of Roman wall. In Deansgate stands a Roman column 30 feet high, discovered during excavations of the Minster in 1969. Possibly it belonged to the fortress' main hall. Roman dignitaries occasionally visited York: two Emperors died here, and here Constantine was proclaimed Emperor. You can see a fine bust of him with other artefacts from this period in the **Yorkshire Museum**. The botanical gardens of the Museum date from the early 19th century; nonchalant peacocks strut among the plants.

By the 6th century the Saxons ruled York, and what remained of the Roman fortress was demolished around 800. Sixty-six years later the town fell to the Vikings. Jorvik, as they called it, became a thriving river port. At the **Jorvik Viking Centre**, opened in 1984, visitors stepping into a remote-

controlled car are transported back to 9th-century Coppergate (street of the coopers or cup-makers) past thatch and wattle buildings, with authentic smells as well as sights. The original house-timbers, exposed at shoulder height, are some of the best preserved in Britain.

The Norsemen left their mark below modern ground level but the achievement of the Normans – York's next rulers – can still be seen on the skyline. **Clifford's Tower** (**121**) stands on the dome-shaped mound that endures from William the Conqueror's York Castle. Rebuilt in stone in 1244–70, it was one of the largest, most advanced towers of its date. Its creator was possibly Henry de Reyns, who also worked on Westminster Abbey. The name may come from Sir Richard Clifford, hanged on the tower in 1322, or from the Clifford family who claimed to be its hereditary constables. It was garrisoned until 1684, when a fire ignited the magazine, blowing up everything except the outer walls. This may have been deliberate, for that night locals toasted the destruction of 'the Minced Pie'. You can stride around the top of this one-time prison, now a roofless shell. It is particularly atmospheric at sunset.

During the 18th century prisoners were gaoled in two of the three imposing buildings facing the mound. Defoe called the **Debtor's Prison** (1701–5) 'stately', but its grandeur was purely cosmetic and inmates occasionally suffocated in overcrowded cells. To its right the **Assize Courts** (1773–7) were designed by the local architect John Carr; two splendid court-rooms are still used. Opposite, the **Female Prison** (1780), together with the Debtor's Prison, has become the **Castle Museum**, the largest popular folk museum in

113 Above: *The ruins of the church of the Benedictine Abbey of St Mary, begun by Abbot Simon de Warwick in 1270 and probably complete by 1300. This view is of the nave north aisle wall, looking towards the north-west pier of the crossing.*

the country. Its reconstructions of period rooms and whole streets are a delight, particularly Kirkgate, with 19th-century shopfronts, cobbles and a hansom cab.

The Normans raised not only fortresses but religious houses too, including **St Mary's Abbey (113)**, founded *c.*1080, the wealthiest Benedictine abbey in northern England. The gracious ruins in the Museum Gardens are part of the elaborate abbey church built *c.*1270. Viewed against a blue sky its arches assume an almost ethereal quality. Every three or four years St Mary's Abbey serves as setting for the York Mystery Plays, first performed in the Middle Ages on the Feast of Corpus Christi. All trades were controlled by guilds, and at York each was responsible for presenting one of 48 plays telling the Biblical story. Also in the Museum Gardens, near the river, is the timber-framed **Hospitium**, once the abbey guest-house.

The old abbey boundary wall, which surrounded the 12-acre estate, leads you to the **King's Manor**, originally the abbot's residence. At the dissolution of the monasteries Henry VIII seized this mellow red-brick building. He later stayed here (with his fifth wife, Catherine Howard), as did Charles I, who temporarily moved the court to York and whose coat of arms surmounts the entrance. You can stroll through the peaceful courtyards, now part of York University, and visit the Huntingdon Room in the north wing to admire the plaster frieze and the chimneypiece. Near the Manor, in Exhibition Square, the **City Art Gallery** contains paintings by (among others) Van Dyck, Reynolds, Sickert and Gwen John.

St Leonard's Place is named after another medieval hospice, one of the

114 Below: *The south façade of the Minster, seen from Duncombe Place. The south transept (c.1230–40) is the earliest part of the exterior; it was gutted by fire in 1984. The buildings to the right of it are the 14th-century Consistory Court, the vestry, and the Zouche Chapel, which extends below the tall window of the south choir transept.*

grandest until Henry VIII suppressed it. On the site of its gateway the **Red House** was built in 1714 for Sir William Robinson, then Lord Mayor of the city, and in 1744 its old cloister was leased to the **Theatre Royal**, which was constructed in the undercroft. St Leonard's Place has York's only neoclassical terrace, including the De Grey Rooms, now the Tourist Information Office. St Leonard's Place joins **High Petergate**, which like **Low Petergate** takes its name from the Minster, the Cathedral of St Peter. Set on the line of the Via Principalis, one of the Roman fortress' main streets, their gabled houses make a pretty foreground to the Minster.

Intersecting these ancient streets and leading towards the great church is **Stonegate** (**122**), along which the building materials were dragged during its construction. Colourful processions took place here in the Middle Ages; the present-day mix of 15th- and 16th-century houses, many with Georgian and Victorian shopfronts, has great charm. Mulberry Hall, once home of the Bishop of Chester, dates from the 15th century. The late-17th-century Old Punch Bowl is one of the city's oldest inns. A narrow alley off Stonegate leads to the remnants of York's oldest dwelling, the two-storeyed Norman House (*c*.1180). Aged signs in Stonegate give clues to former businesses: a crouching red devil above the entrance to Coffee Yard signals a printer (whose 'devils' were boys who fetched type for their master); on the corner of Minster Gates the goddess Minerva reclines with her owl on a pile of books (**123**), indicating an area of booksellers.

King Edwin was baptised in the first church dedicated to St Peter in 627 where now the Minster looms. The cathedral has been destroyed and rebuilt many times over its 13 centuries. In 1069 flames swept the city and a year later Archbishop Thomas of Bayeux began rebuilding on the flattened

Inside the Minster:
115 (below) *The choir screen, designed in the 1470s and finished in the early 16th century, incorporates statues of all the kings of England from William I to Henry VI.*
116 (right) *The west window, 75 feet high, is renowned for its superb stone tracery, which has given it the name 'the Heart of Yorkshire'. It was probably the work of Ivo de Raughton, and was donated by Archbishop Melton, who also gave the glass. This is the work of Master Robert, whose contract enables the window to be dated to 1338.*

remains of the Roman fortress. Another fire in 1137 led to major alterations. More changes followed in 1220 under the auspices of Archbishop Walter de Grey. In 1829 one Jonathan Martin hid in the cathedral after Evensong and set light to the choir. This was not discovered until the following morning and not extinguished until that night. By then it had caused terrible destruction. Another fire in 1840 raged in the south-west tower. The nave collapsed; the west doors were virtually destroyed. In 1967 evidence showed that the Minster was in danger of collapsing. Two million pounds was raised to lay new foundations and brace the piers of the central towers. Then on 9 July 1984 lightning struck and ignited a fire which damaged the famous rose window in the south transept. Renovation began again.

Although it is England's largest medieval church, the Minster does not dominate York. Walking around the exterior helps you appreciate its immensity. Internally it is 486 feet long, and the central tower is 198 feet high. On the north side the view is interrupted by the late-13th-century octagonal chapter house, the largest in England, with massive buttresses, a beautiful medieval wooden ceiling and exquisitely carved stalls.

The Minster has the widest medieval nave in England but the slender piers enhance its loftiness. A figure of St Peter stands between the two central west doors, below the 14th-century 'Heart of Yorkshire', the 75-foot-high west window (**116**) with superb stone tracery and panels filled with grisaille (uncoloured) glass. There is grisaille too in the five lancets of the north transept's north wall, known collectively as the Five Sisters Window (*c.*1250). Charles Dickens, fascinated by this window, invented a tale of five siblings

117 Above: *When it was first built, in 1877, York station was held to be the largest in Europe. Thomas Prosser designed this magnificent curved train shed, 800 feet long, its roof supported by slender Corinthian columns.*

118 Right: *Still a major centre of Britain's railway network, York is now the home of the National Railway Museum. The steam locomotive shown here is the London Brighton and South Coast Railway Class A tank 'Boxhill' (1880).*

whose tapestries were copied in glass as a memorial to the youngest who had died. The window was restored in the 1920s in tribute to women of the Empire who died in World War I. It was reworked with lead from nearby Rievaulx Abbey which had been buried since the dissolution of the monasteries.

In the south transept (*c.*1220–40), the earliest visible part of the Minster above ground, the rose window boasts early-16th-century glass and commemorates the marriage of Henry VII and Elizabeth of York (1486), which ended the Wars of the Roses. Here too is the 13th-century tomb of Walter de Grey. A life-sized painting of the Archbishop was found on the coffin lid when it was removed during restoration in 1968. Inside the tomb lay a ring with a huge uncut sapphire and the Archbishop's chalice, paten and pectoral staff.

An asymmetrical screen (**115**), built *c.*1475–1506, flanks the entrance to the choir. Its niches hold sculptures of the kings of England from William I to Henry VI – all original save that of Henry VI, which was removed lest it become a shrine to the murdered monarch.

The east window in the Lady Chapel is the world's largest surviving single expanse of medieval glass, the work of John Thornton of Coventry. God appears in the central light at the top and the Bishop of Durham who paid for it kneels at the base.

The undercroft contains the cathedral treasury, and a museum (created

119 Above: *The Shambles, one of the oldest thoroughfares in the city, is mentioned by name in the Domesday Book (1086).*

120 Right: *Walmgate Bar has the only complete town's barbican in England. The parallel walls were built out at right angles to the city walls, ending in a gateway with a portcullis.*

during recent restoration work) which traces York's history. In the crypt a font stands on the traditional site of the first York Minster above the well in which Edwin was baptised, and beneath a wooden trap-door you can glimpse a column base belonging to the Roman building which once stood here. Also on view are a 12th-century Doomstone, a Norman carving depicting hell, and a Byzantine-style Virgin and Child.

The graceful Norman arcade in the Minster precincts may have been part of a cloister in the former Archbishop's Palace, destroyed three hundred years ago when Archbishop Young sold the lead of the great hall's roof to buy an estate for his son. The current Archbishop lives at Bishopthorpe, about 2 miles away. Near to the arcade is the Minster Library, accommodated in a 13th-century chapel and open to the public. Pass the Deanery and come to the **Treasurer's House**, largely built in the 17th century and now National Trust property. It has a fine drawing-room and dining-room and a charming garden. Behind the back façade of adjoining Gray's Court are the 12th-century remains of the original Treasurer's House.

St William's College (**126**), built in 1465 on a courtyard plan, once lodged the Minster's chantry priests. Its long half-timbered upper storey hangs over the ashlar ground floor. In Charles I's reign it housed the royal printing press. Above the outer doorway sits the figure of St William and under the eaves are carved figures of the Virgin and Child and of St Christopher.

College Street joins the curving Goodramgate, where a line of enchanting cottages, Our Lady's Row (1316), was built to endow a chantry of the Virgin Mary at the adjacent church of **Holy Trinity**. Small and dark, this still contains 17th- and 18th-century box pews and its 15th-century tower has a rare saddleback roof. The oldest ecclesiastical building in York is the tower of **St Mary's Church** in Bishophill Junior: its 10th-century base is made with re-used Roman materials.

One of the most famous of York's many splendid churches is **All Saints Pavement**, Coppergate Walk, whose lantern tower is a 19th-century reproduction of the original which guided medieval travellers towards the city. All Saints has strong associations with the city's guilds, and in January the annual service of the Merchant Adventurers' Company is held here. Founded in 1357 as a religious institution – the Guild of our Lord and the Blessed Virgin – this Company came to be dominated by mercers, and played an important role in the city's commercial life, especially in the early 15th century, when the cloth trade was at its peak. The **Merchant Adventurer's Hall**, decked with portraits and banners, is still used for meetings. The oldest part – the 14th-century undercroft – used to be a hospital for poor members of the Company. At its far end lies the austerely impressive Trinity Chapel (1368). The other rooms are furnished mainly with 17th-century English oak.

Notable early domestic buildings include **Bowes Morrell House** in Walmgate, a late-14th-century timber-framed building restored in 1966 and, south-west of the River Ouse, **Jacob's Well**, a modest property sporting an intriguing 15th-century canopied porch with carved heads. The church nearby in Micklegate, **Holy Trinity**, was part of a priory founded in 1089. A casualty of the fire of 1137, the church was rebuilt a century later. You can still see the cruel stocks in the churchyard.

Tucked away on this same side of the river, but not to be missed, is **All Saints North Street**. Carved angels throng its chancel and chancel aisle

121 *Standing on the motte of William the Conqueror's castle is Clifford's Tower, a keep rebuilt in stone at the instigation of Henry II in 1244. In design it is one of the largest and most advanced towers of its date, unusual in its quatrefoil shape. It contained a hall, and had a chapel over the entrance. It seems to have been strongly defended – arrow slits and gun ports can be seen in the outer walls. However, much of its life was spent in a state of disrepair; in 1360 it was described as cracked from top to bottom, and the huge crack is still visible (to the right of the side shown here), with an infill of differently coloured stone.*

KLEIBER'S COURT
TEA ROOMS AND COFFEE SHOP

HIGH PETERGATE
MINSTER GATES
ALPHA NOVA
ALPHA NOVA
ALPHA NOVA

roofs. Though predominantly 15th century in style, the church has Roman masonry and is renowned for its early stained glass. In the lower right hand corner of the glowing Nine Orders of Angels window (south aisle) you can spot a man in spectacles. **St Martin cum Gregory** also has fascinating glass. Here the tower plinth is of Roman stone, from the Temple of Mithras which stood opposite the gate. In the north aisle is some plain glass with a patriotic message scratched soon after the Jacobite Rebellion (1745): 'I hope this may be a plase for true protestants to resort to & never to be ruled by Papists God Bless King George ye 2d & Billy off Cumberland Whome God long preserve.'

The first mention of a Guildhall on the present site north-east of the river dates from 1378. The **Guildhall** seen today is a reconstruction of the original (1446–8), which was reduced to a shell during an air raid in 1942. You get the best view of its position on the waterfront from the three-arched Ouse Bridge (1810–21). A bridge has always forded the river at this point: a new one had to be built in 1154 when the existing structure collapsed under the vast crowds who turned out to greet the return from exile of Archbishop William.

In the 18th century York became a social centre for the northern gentry and at this time the **Mansion House**, official residence of the Lord Mayor, was built (1725–30). Its exterior bears the city's coat of arms; its banqueting hall and state room have period furnishings. York's **Assembly Rooms** (1732) were designed by the Palladian architect Lord Burlington. The splendid central hall has 52 Corinthian pillars, but not everyone approved: Sarah Churchill, Duchess of Marlborough, complained that the pillars were so close it was impossible to pass between them in a hooped evening dress.

The streets of York:
122 (left) *Stonegate, on the lines of the Roman Via Praetoria. As the principal approach to the Minster, which can be glimpsed at the top of the street in this view, it was often used by processions of civic dignitaries on their way from the Guildhall.*
123 (below left) *The junction of Stonegate and Minster Gates with High Petergate, presided over by John Wolstenholme's carving (1801) of Minerva and her owl.*
124 (below right) *The pleasant open space of King's Square, amidst the narrow lanes in the centre of the city.*

YORK
DIOCESAN
BOARD OF FINANCE

125 Left: *Georgian York was the social capital of the north of England, and the city is full of excellent 18th-century domestic architecture. These four doorways are a sample of the innumerable rewarding details that enliven a walk through the centre.*

126 Above: *St William's College, built on a courtyard plan like the colleges of Oxford and Cambridge, was originally (1465) the home of the Minster's chantry priests. Having changed hands several times, it now serves Diocesan purposes once more.*

Public transport in the 18th and 19th centuries used local inns as stopping-points. A great coaching centre, York was full of inns like the famous George in Coney Street, which stood where Leak & Thorp is now. (Charlotte and Anne Brontë stayed here in 1849.) Coaches left this hostelry for Hull, Manchester and Newcastle, braving highwaymen like Dick Turpin and John Revison. A main thoroughfare for hundreds of years, Coney Street is still watched over by the 'Little Admiral', who has crowned the great clock of **St Martin le Grand** since 1688. He used to rotate, his sextant following the sun, but a World War II bomb disabled him.

York's elegant residences include the beautifully restored Fairfax House in Castlegate (1755–6), designed by John Carr, and Castlegate House (also by Carr) which stands opposite. The finely timbered Herbert House, a rare early-17th-century survivor, is situated in the **Pavement**, a market place first recorded *c.*1329. Here public gatherings, punishments and executions happened. Branching off it is an eerily narrow alley, Lady Peckitt's Yard, named after a Lord Mayor's wife and, it is easy to imagine, a haven for cut-purses. On the Pavement's other side, the shortest of streets enjoys the longest of names: Whipmawhopmagate. This connects to York's most celebrated street, the **Shambles** (**119**), where butchers traditionally had their 'shamnels' or stalls. At No. 35 a shrine commemorates butcher's wife Margaret Clitherow, pressed to death in 1586 for harbouring Jesuits and canonised in 1970. Today a lone butcher remains, and antiques and crafts are the fare now offered by this picturesque area to the crowds of visitors.